Gypsy Cards
The Enchantment

Rodrigo Petrosky

Illustrated by Anastasia Globa

Copyright © 2019

All rights reserved. This book or any portion thereof may not be reproduced or used in any manner whatsoever without the express written permission of the author except for the use of brief quotations in a book review.

Card and cover images by Anastasia Globa

Printed in Australia
First Printing, 2019
ISBN: 978-0-6484104-6-1

White Light Publishing
Melton, VIC, Australia 3337
whitelightpublishing.com.au

This book is dedicated to all my ancestors, from Russia, Romani and Brazil. For all the victims of persecution and discrimination and especially for a very special soul who inspires me, someone who I will meet on Earth or on the Spiritual Path.

Magic encounters of all ancestors
From the remote travels, lands crossed
From the capital of the fertile land
From the place of tsars
From crossing the world
Finally met in Aboriginal land
From the taste of the Andes
Magic creates life
A life that will be always
An open heart

Contents

Introduction - The Journey	7
Who are the Gypsies?	9
What does it mean to be a Gypsy?	11
The Gypsies today	12
Gypsy Spirituality	13
The Origin of Gypsy Cards	16
Understanding the Cards	18
The Suits (minor arcana)	19
Numbers	21
Consecrating Your Deck	21
Performing a reading	23
Increasing your Clairvoyance and Intuition	24
Final Considerations	26
Spreads	27
One Card – Yes/No	28
Two Card Spread	30
Three Card Spread	31
Five Card Spread – The Wheel of Fortune	32
Celtic Cross	33
The Gypsy Mandala Spread	35
The Gypsy Spread	37
The Cards Index	39
Card Combinations	147
About the Author	239
About the Illustrator	239
Bibliography	241

Introduction - The Journey

The Gypsy Cards are extremely popular in Latin America, Portugal, Spain and France. They take you on a journey full of enchantment that has been passed along generations. Gypsy Cards have influenced the lives of many people, some of them very well known. There are many theories explaining the origin of the cards even before Madame Lenormand printed the first deck. The Gypsy Deck is simple and assertive in a way that can easily answer simple questions to a complex reading.

In the Anglophonic world there is very little material published on the Gypsy Cards, mainly due to the tarot being the preference of many. There is limited material written in English, and much of it has incorrect information and gives a wrong conception about Gypsy people, including spirituality, the origin of the cards and even "Gypsy spells" prescribed. So many misconceptions have led me to believe that many people do not know who the Gypsies really are. Many of the ideas come from documentaries broadcast on television and include a great deal of racist content. I was presented with a decision to write this book which arose from my journey.

From my early childhood I was surrounded by spirituality, oracles, shamanism and the Gypsy community. I was born in Brazil and come from a bloodline of different Gypsy groups, Cale, Russian, Native American and Portuguese. The Gypsies were always part of my life, and even though my family did not live in Gypsy camps or caravans, we often visited their camps where we would participate in events, witnessing and learning oracles from an early age. I chose to follow an academic life and even joined the military when I grew up, which is very unusual for a Gypsy. I have lived in several countries and had various forms of employment but have always offered my oracles on the side. Taking part in many holistic events, I noticed that there are no Gypsy Cards available at these festivals and have not been able to find any in bookstores.

On my last trip to Brazil, a friend Kralissa, a Bona Dichera (street palm reader) looked in my eyes and said, "You are part of us, you can write, you need to educate the Gaje (Non-Gypsies) about us." At same time I noticed that my friend Nicholas Ramanuch, the only Gypsy anthropologist I know of, was releasing a few different books, clarifying aspects, breaking myths and explaining our traditions and our history to Portuguese speakers. I was amazed, I felt I had an obligation to do something about it, as all the stories about us, our spirituality, our traditions were always written by non-Gypsies.
I started to read more about what was published and I was shocked by the literature and public knowledge about us. I come across people who call

themselves Gypsies, people who claim to talk to Gypsy spirits and so much misleading information. I felt I had no choice and decided to write this book; however, I did not know how, I have always been busy with clinical work, events, conferences and professional development. I allocated one hour per day, intending to complete this book within 2 years. As I started writing, the excitement flew through my veins and I started to sacrifice my sleep and completed the first draft in one month. I had one problem though, I had no illustrations for the cards. I am not a gifted drawer and I did not think the existing cards represented the images Romani people see. My long-term friend Anastasia took care of the illustration, with some majestic work that represents exactly what the Romani people mean and the meaning of each card, thank you Anastasia. Thanks also to Natalia Pedan for using your intuitive eye to add some final touches to the book.

This book will explain who the Gypsies are and tell you about Gypsy spirituality. It will also provide basic information to understand the cards, detailed information for each card and teach you reading methods, Gypsy rituals for the cards and how you can improve your intuition. For the first time the Gypsy Cards are explained by a Gypsy person.

The Gypsy Card deck is available for purchase at whitelightshop.com

Who are the Gypsies?

There are many theories and myths about gypsies, some with a certain logic, some absurd and some even spiritual. Imagine a world where people have no fixed address, documents, bank account, passport, or history. And let their lives go unnoticed, as if they did not exist. That the only certainty is that you will never lack prejudice and ignorance, fear and fascination, injustices and joys along your endless journey.

The Gypsy universe is so ancient and extensive, so full of beliefs and stories that not even its own people know the boundary between truth and legend. It is that the name "gypsy" designates many peoples spread by almost all regions of the world. People with different colours, beliefs, religions, customs, rituals, which, for reasons sometimes difficult to understand, were sheltered under this immense umbrella. The English term *Gypsy* (or *Gipsy*) originates from the Middle English *Gypcian*, short for *Egyptian*. The Spanish term *Gitano* and French *Gitan* have similar etymologies. The Portuguese call *Gypsy*. They are ultimately derived from the Greek *Aigyptioi*, meaning Egyptian, via Latin. The word *Gypsy* in English has become so pervasive that many Romani organizations use it in their own organizational names.

The history of the gypsies is all based on assumptions. And the reason is simple: documents are missing. Gypsies are a non-writing people. They never left any records that could explain their origins and customs. Their traditions are conveyed orally, but neither do they make much of a question - Gypsies live today, are not interested in any vestiges of the past. The difficulty of settling, the almost non-existent concept of property and the way they deal with death - eliminating all the deceased's belongings - making further in-depth research work even more difficult.

From the observation of the similarity between the Romani languages (practiced by the Roms, the largest of the gypsy groups) and Hindi (Sanskrit variation, practiced in northwest India), it was possible to elucidate the first and greatest gypsy diaspora. A genetic map has corroborated with the Indian heritage. A large contingent, possibly by a caste of warriors, would have abandoned India in the eleventh century, when the Persian sultan invaded and dominated the north of the country. Then they emigrated to Persia, Russia and arrived in the Balkans. The nomadic nature of many gypsy groups, however, also allows us to assume a natural immigration movement that has arrived in Europe as its cities developed, offering business opportunities for all sorts of travellers and pilgrims.

Studies say that by the fifteenth century, they had passed through Egypt. At least it was from there that they said to come to who asked their origin. The term Gypsy is still pejorative, however modern society calls them Gypsy when there are adventurous, travel passionate, move around, open minded and spiritual. It is interesting how some people call themselves Gypsies; However it is vital to understand who Gypsies are. There is also confusion with Irish Travellers in United Kingdom, who are not Romani. Since countries have passports, immigration control and restrictions on caravans, most of Romani people are settled in countries all over the world, living in permanent addresses. But before that, even in the thirteenth century, a document written by the Patriarch of Constantinople already warned of the presence of the adingánous, a wandering people who, he said, taught diabolical things. This record is the first to treat the gypsies pejoratively and to register the fear that the European cities felt of their caravans. It was the beginning of gypsy fate.

"From the outset of contact with the West, they have been the cause of conflicts, provoking disorder and subversive to the system. And they suffered all sorts of religious, cultural, political and racial persecutions, " according to Aluízio Azevedo, a master of gypsy history. It is hard to know what came first: unorthodox habits or prejudice against such a different culture. The Gypsies had dark skin, many children, an indecipherable tongue and unknown origin. Perhaps the lack of job opportunities has been the cause of their artistic fate. They were driven away and then moved, bringing news of where they came from. Thus, came the fame of magicians, sorcerers and wizards. If everyone believed in this, why not take advantage to make money? And then the women read the hands and oracles, something they had already learned before the diaspora. Trading objects was another way of surviving: gypsies had access to "exotic" goods and could take their stuff wherever they went.

Watching the European pilgrims, who easily moved in and out of the cities, they copied the idea of safe conduct - a kind of passport father. They justified the nomadic life by saying that bishops had condemned them for seven years as a penance for the abandonment of the Christian faith. Some of the saved conducts allowed even those who did not give alms to steal. A tactic to increase the chance of being accepted into communities, doing business, and displaying your artistic gifts. Until the farce was over, and they jumped again to another city.

During the Christian Reconquest of 1492, in the Iberian Peninsula, Arabs, Jews and Gypsies were expelled - many of them came to the Americas. A century later, they were swept from France, and from England by Henry VIII. Later, Queen Elizabeth I decreed that being a Gypsy was a crime punishable by death. They were deported with the convicts to Australia. One of the legends that emerged at this time, and which continues to this day, is that one of the blacksmiths who made the nails that held Jesus on the cross was a gypsy. So his people would have been cursed with a nomadic life. And in this way, the image of a wandering, mystical, dangerous and **controversial** people was constructed. Thus, in the contact with the images constructed and fed in the West, the concept of a gypsy town was created.

What does it mean to be a Gypsy?

Defining gypsy identity is a lot harder than it looks. Subdivided into 3 main ethnic groups (Rom, Cale and Sinti), they do not constitute a homogenous people. Not everyone is nomadic, not everyone speaks Romani, not everyone dances around campfires wearing colourful clothes, some are poor and others are wealthy. What makes them a people is a common feeling of not being Gajes - as they call non-gypsies - and of identifying themselves as Rom, Cale or Sinti.

In spite of all the divergences, some characteristics allow drawing a common profile of these groups. The first of these is the traveling spirit; although not all are nomads, the gypsies do not feel they belong to a single place. They do not take root, do not have a concrete notion of property - they are always doing business with their belongings, preferably in gold, which does not lose any value and is accepted in any nation (hence the gypsy image is linked to the use of gold as a prop, especially on the teeth of women). They do not like to submit to laws and rules other than their own. Above all, they value freedom. Thus, they may even settle for a long time in one place (as is common among the Sinti). In this case, they seek to live on the same street or, preferably, in camps where they can preserve their autonomy and maintain family unity - another primordial aspect of gypsy life.

It is around the family that a gypsy community organizes itself. There is a leader, always a man, who is appointed by merit and not by inheritance. He is chosen by taking into account several aspects. One of them, which is important for renting land, setting up a circus or participating in fairs, is having an identity document, which has become a real challenge. He must also be a good interlocutor between the government and his group, as well as having the ability to solve the internal problems of the camp. It is he who dictates the rules, divides the tasks, creates the laws of the group. Gypsies cannot register the birth of children because they do not have their own documents, it is an endless process.

Gypsy society is patriarchal. In marrying, the man becomes responsible for the sustenance of the home. The wife moves in with her husband's family and must take care of him, the in-laws, the house and the children. Cousin marriage continues to be encouraged in an attempt to preserve the family nucleus. In nomadic communities, it is more difficult to have a marriage between gypsies and Gajes, although it is possible and permitted. In this case, the Gaje, male or female, must change their life. Being a gypsy does not depend on blood - if a Gaje chooses to join the group, they automatically become one of them.

As they settled in Europe and the Americas, the Gypsies assimilated ceremonies and Western rites, but some Gypsy traditions remain strong. The symbology of death is the main one. The Cale perform healing rituals as soon as the disease is diagnosed. Besides accepting traditional medicine, they resort to prayers, chains of prayers, bottles of herbs, teas and sympathies, usually given by a healer of the group. During the wake, the dead person is the centre of the ritual and, depending on the position he occupied, a new leadership may have to be elected and the family is restructured. The body of the deceased is washed, anointed with aromatic herbs and dressed properly. This moment of suffering and complicity is important for the identity of the group. As in other cultures, the possibility of transcendence is perceived. In the case of Gypsies, this is the time to find your soul naturally traveling. In some camps, all belongings of the deceased are eliminated, even your caravan gets burned. It's like a cut in history, nothing is guarded, the past is not redeemed. After a member's death, many gypsy groups move to a new camp.

The Gypsies today

It is estimated that there are 15 million Romani around the world. Like everything related to this universe, this is just an estimate - they live on the margins of society and do not usually participate in demographic census surveys. The gypsies have been treated as outcasts since the 15th century. Until the 19th century, they were enslaved in the region known today as Romania. During World War II, they were persecuted by the Nazis and according to some historians were the most decimated people by the Holocaust. Of the 1 million Roma living in Europe, 500,000 were murdered. Many of the survivors emigrated to the United States.

The first group of gypsies to arrive in Brazil, mostly Cale, arrived there in the 16th century after being deported from Portugal. The Roms came voluntarily from the middle of the eighteenth century. At that time, they were itinerant traders of slaves, horses and handicrafts. Today they buy and sell cars, televisions and towels. In more recent times, the sometimes very poor Roms came from Eastern Europe to Brazil. Although some Gypsies remain in one location these days, most remain in itinerant life. Many Gypsy orphans were adopted by Gajes which increased miscegenation. The majority of Gypsy people are performers, artists or work in crafts, jewellery making, oracle reading and woodwork. Although illiteracy among Roma is high, there are a great number of Gypsies who are educated and well-integrated in society. Lack of study and marginalized life pushed many further into crime, fuelling the pervasive visions that have survived since the first contact between Roma and Europeans. Until they are understood, they will keep moving and start all over again, they will continue living their gypsy saga.

Today the prejudice continues, fortunately on a much smaller scale than in years gone by, but the lack of knowledge about Romanis and the discrimination still exists. Most Gypsy children now go to school, and marriages with non-Gypsies are increasing. The downside of that is that the millennial traditions are no longer passed on to the next generations – to be free like birds, believing that the Earth is a space for every living being, and that people should not be limited to the country where they are born. For every country Gypsies travelled to, they assimilated many things into their own traditions as well as donating the Romani influence on the places they stopped at. It is evidenced in folk dances and music such as flamenco and something very simple and beautiful as camping and travelling in caravans.

Gypsies have always been resilient through the way they have been treated as their belief that people should not own land remains strong. The World is our temporary country, and just another place to travel to as the spiritual life continues.

Gypsy Spirituality

Gypsies are essentially Masters of mysticism and nature, which incorporates astrology, reading signs and symbols associated with spiritual visions and interpretations. Their spirituality is often compared to shamanism, in rituals, dances, clairvoyance and oracles. All knowledge is passed from parents to their children.

Romanis predominantly follow the religion of the country they live in. They can be Catholic in Latin America, Muslim in Turkey, Christian Orthodox in Romania and Russia, Hindu in India and so it goes on. However, they do not follow these religions strictly and neither do they accept their dogmas. There are aspects that are taken into consideration; they try to be sure not to offend the people (their religion) of the country they are in. They believe in reincarnation and in clairvoyance, **however they do not believe another spirit can take over one who is living.**

Gypsy key beliefs are:

1) Monotheistic (single god). These beliefs are mixed with certain characteristics of Zoroastrianism, the cult of fire, because this cult of Persia was acquired by the Gypsies when they were there for many centuries.
2) Belief in a spiritual world, where there are pure and impure spirits.
3) Permanent struggle between Good and Evil.
4) Death as a passage to the spiritual realm, where the spirit of the dead is impure in its journey. Their kinsmen and their material possessions are also unclean during the period of mourning.
5) Notion of marimê - what is impure, or subject to impurities and vuzhô - pure. This is similar to the Hebrew notion of kosher, with the meaning contrary to the impure, or ritually pure.
6) Rituals of marriage, and proof of virginity (in traditional communities); funerals and birth.

Rom are strong believers in amulets and talismans, and that items carried in one's pocket - a coin, a stone - become imbued with the characteristics of the carrier. These are referred to as "pocket deities," and it is said that certain objects are automatically conferred great power – shells, daggers and crystals.

Amongst some Romani tribes, animals and birds are attributed divinatory and prophetic powers. Birds seem to be popular in these tales; they are considered bringers of luck and horses are also considered magical - the skull of a horse is said to keep ghosts out of their caravan or home. The deep love Gypsies have for animals is not reflected through pet ownership. They use horses as a transport, but in most cases Gypsies believe animals need to live according to their natural destiny. Building a co-dependent relationship with an animal and depriving them to live their nature is considered selfish and disabling. As Gypsies are obsessive about cleanliness of their homes, having animals inside is considered muchane (dirty), however contemporary Romanies have pets inside the house.

Water is considered a source of great magical power. It is lucky to meet a woman carrying a full jug of water, but bad luck if the jug is empty. It is a custom to pay homage to the blessing of water after filling a jug or a bucket, by spilling a few drops on the ground as an offering. In fact, it is considered rude - and even dangerous - to take a drink of water without first paying tribute.

There is a considerate amount of literature about clairvoyants teaching gypsy magic, however, **gypsy magic does not exist**. Spells are performed in offerings for gratitude, abundance and health. They should never ever be used to change another person's free will, such as love spells to make a person fall in love or to bring a lover back. Following one God, family values, life as a spiritual journey, nature symbols, and intuition are all important aspects of the Gypsy people. In Brazilian shamanism and in spiritualistic religions such as Umbanda and Candomblé, Gypsy themed rituals are performed and they refer to Gypsy spiritual mentors as guides.

The Origin of Gypsy Cards

It is believed that the Gypsy deck was constituted from innumerable sciences being the result of a sum of knowledge from the gypsy symbols, game cards, tarot, numerology and cabal. There are several theories of how the first gypsy deck appeared; with tales that come from as far back as the first millennium. According to tales, it is believed that the gypsy children made drawings of what they observed and passed from parents to children. Legend says that in Russia a gypsy named Zemfira presented the first cards, but all the drawings were destroyed.

Gypsies have always been masters of oracles - from Indian coins, playing cards, crystal ball and tarot, yet they have never published any packets. We can find in the Gypsy deck definite images of man's strong connection with nature, simple objects, natural phenomena, animals and, in a general way, the influence that these forces have on his life, and the synthesis of people who respect and believe in the manifestations of the Universe. It was adopted by the Roma people due to familiarity with the symbols and to be assertive. The Lenormand decks along with the Tarot cards are the most used in the field of card reading, extremely popular in Brazil, but little known in the Anglophone world. Given the symbols and the interpretation of dreams that is an old gypsy practice and later corroborated by Jung, one can also interpret the images from dreams and the cards.

The Gypsy cards were codified by Madame Marie-Anne Adelaide Lenormand, a French fortune-teller of great renown who also performed, besides other divinatory activities, palmistry, clairvoyance, reading cards, reading tea leaves, astrology among other oracles. Lenormand had among her clients Josephine de Beauharnais, wife of Napoleon Bonaparte. She would have predicted the rise and fall of Emperor Napoleon, the secrets of Empress Josephine, and the fate of many notables of her time. She was born in Alençon, Normandy. She lost her father when she was only one year old and her mother when she was just five years old, after which she was sent to live in a convent. There came the first reports of her clairvoyance. She spent a lot of time with the gypsy people who were discriminated against all, seeking to help them and learning much of their culture.

She lived in Paris in the period subsequent to the French Revolution and there consolidated her reputation of clairvoyance. In 1807, Lenormand read in Napoleon's hands his intention to divorce Josefina. To get her away he sent her to prison for 12 days. This fact was the true launch of her career and she became the most popular fortune teller of her time. For unknown reasons, the secrets of the Tarot Lenormand temporarily disappeared with her death, and about 50 years later they were recovered with the discovery of some manuscripts. From these documents two decks were developed, one of them known as the Lenormand deck which was illustrated with images of the time. The other was illustrated with simpler and more modern images and corresponded to the version used by the gypsies, propagators of this pack.

The "Sibila de Alençon" deck was first published in 1828 and had 52 cards, the same as an ordinary deck of playing cards. This set was redesigned and reduced to 36 letters by 1840, as requested by the Grimaud printing house. This smaller set was known as Little Lenormand. As already happened with the deck of Etteila several engravings were added to the numbered letters. It was used more for the popular card reading, as it facilitates attribution of practical meanings to the cards. This measure on one hand makes it easier to relate to the reader, but on the other limits the symbolic amplitude. The popularity of the Lenormand deck has stimulated countless copies and imitations throughout Europe and to this day is redesigned and published differently, but never by a gypsy person, until now.

Understanding the Cards

Before you learn about reading the cards, it is very important to understand the impact of the cards, the numbers and how the deck was put together. Similar to the Tarot, the Gypsy Deck is a journey of a life, that comes in the form of animals, simple objects, plants, nature, constructions, numbers and equivalent minor arcana. It is important to understand that similar cards in the Gypsy Deck does not necessarily mean they are the same.

All cards should be interpreted in a holistic way, everything is important, the colours, the expressions, the numbers and both the major and minor arcana.

Everything matters when reading cards, the major arcana is the main part, but the minor arcana is also relevant in different situations, the number, the image and most importantly: the intuition.

Major arcana is depicted by the central figures/images and symbolizes our learning and more complex issues that need to be worked out internally. It also represents the awareness of the moment we are experiencing.

Minor arcana is depicted with conventional card symbols and represents collective subconsciousness, our mental patters and beliefs.

The Suits (minor arcana)

Clubs (Wands)

The suit of Clubs relates to the Fire element and is grouped as cards that govern growth, self-development, creativity, ingenuity, energy, ideas, inspiration, passion.

Hearts (Cups)

The suit of Hearts relates to the Water element, God's love and the world of feelings, love, dreams, fantasies, artistic and psychic connections.

Spades (Swords)

The suit of Spades relates to the Air element, and symbolizes form and matter, in particular the logical and rational mind. This suit can also symbolise instability, dispute, struggle and/or search for truth. Usually this suit sends an ominous message.

Diamonds (Pentacles or Coins)

The suit of Diamonds relates to the Earth Element and these cards represent physical expression, money, work and materiality.

Numbers

Numerology is just as important as any other science; numbers did not appear by mistake, nor simply just for the purpose of counting. Renowned philosophers and mathematicians already knew the importance of numbers in order to understand the evolution and the individual journey according to the vibration of each number. Numbers go from 1 to 9 with zero being a neutral number, and bigger numbers are solely sequential. The Gypsy Cards follow the same journey, from 1 to 36 (3+6=9). Although numerology is a complex science that requires a great deal of study, only the basics will be outlined here to help you understand the cards. There is a vast amount of literature available should you wish to study it further.

After number 9, all of the numbers should be added together in order to reduce it to a single digit. For example: 77 (7+7=14): (1+4=5). Five is the final number. However, the vibration of each number is not the same, for example: 12 (1+2=3) does not have the same vibration and order as the 21(2+1=3). Although it is the same number – 3 - the context is different, as number 1 followed by 2 is a beginning and 2 followed by 1 is a retrograde. Also, there are three double digit numbers that are not reducible. 11, 22 and 33 are known as Master Numbers. These are very powerful numbers and, in this case, number 11 is not 1+1=2. 11 is the Visionary Master, 22 is the Builder Master and 33 is the Master of Unconditional Love. Below is the basic meaning of each single digit number:

1) Courage, start, determination, new and individual.
2) Alliances, pregnancy, duality, giving nature and sharing.
3) Balance, birth, expansion, manifest, expansion and solidity.
4) Structure, boredom, order, construction and isolation.
5) Arts, sensitivity, changes, experience, sexuality and changes.
6) Responsibility, negativity, relationships, affection and fear.
7) Spirituality, enlightenment, wisdom, self-development, awakening and transformation.
8) Infinity, possibilities, rewards, luck, rewards and power.
9) Wisdom, experience, purification, spirituality, maturity and endings.

Consecrating Your Deck

When you acquire a deck of Gypsy Cards, consecration is the first thing to do. Please do not use your cards as soon as you open the pack, a valid reading only happens after you have blessed your cards. If you are doing readings for other people, it is advisable to have a separate deck to the one you use for yourself. The Gypsy cards are a tool to connect humans, nature and divine energy. All the knowledge is concentrated in the energy of respect, love, harmony and balance. When you consecrate your cards you are instantly putting your energy into it, the Universe's vibes and spiritual healing as well as opening paths for the light and all of that will bring harmony during the readings. There are many different ways to consecrate your deck. Below is one example of how Romanis do so in South America and the Iberian Peninsula. It is simple, and you only have to do it at once for each deck.

You will need
A dagger
A yellow candle
One glass of water (as pure as possible)
7 crystals
A bouquet of flowers
A white, golden or purple scarf
3 valid coins
One glass of red wine
Sage incense

During an evening of a First Quarter or New Moon, find a peaceful place to make a small altar. Place the scarf on the ground or table with the deck in the centre of it with the crystals around the deck. Burn the incense and focus your energy on cleaning the aura and environment. The dagger increases the mental power and cuts all negativity. The flowers represent happiness and peace and the candle represents the divine fire, the light, the wisdom and balance. These can be placed at the corners of the altar.

Pass each card, one by one, over the incense and then place them in the centre of the altar in the form of a fan with the pictures facing up. It is important to hold gratitude in your heart and maintain focus on the task at hand for the entire time. Ask for the angels and good spirits to be present. Choose a prayer of your choice to be said as you perform the ritual. You can use the following prayer to St. Sara Kali if you wish. I have provided it in both Romani and English.

Romani

Manglimos Katar e Santa Sara Kali
Tu Ke San Pervo Icana Romli Anelumia
Tu Ke Biladiato Le Gajie Anassogodi Guindiças
Tu Ke daradiato Le Gajie,
Tai Chudiato Anemaria Thie Meres Bi Paiesco
Tai Bocotar Janes So Si e Dar, E Bock,
Thai O Duck Ano Iló Thiena Mekes Murre Dusmaia Thie Açal Manda
Thai Thie Bilavelma Thie Aves Murri Dukata Angral O Dhiel Thie Dhiesma Bar, Sastimôs
Thai Thie Blagois Murrô Traio Thie Diel O Dhiel.

English

You are the only Holy Gypsy in the World.
You suffered all forms of humiliation and prejudice.
You that you were frightened and thrown overboard.
So that you die of thirst and hunger.
You know what fear, hunger, heartache, and pain in the heart are.
Do not let my enemies mock me or mistreat me.
Holy Mary, may you be my advocate before God.
May You give me luck, health and bless my life.
Amen

Gypsy Invocation

Hold the dagger above the cards and cut the air.
To all powerful spirits and helping souls, please turn this sacred oracle and bless me with light for me to be in service of love, wisdom and knowledge between humankind and the Universe. Turn me into a facilitator of the divine messages bringing full conscious knowledge of souls and divination. Fulfil me with the power of the sacred fire and the pure magic of all elements. These Gypsy Cards may be the tool to change what has to be changed, relieve the pain of the ones who suffer and clarify all the questions on the eternal moment of now. I ask that the divine virtue of peace be present in order of me to do good and show care. I invoke the happiness, the loving energy and the light of wisdom for the truth and the sacred path. That these cards may conduct my heart, body, mind and spirit for the divine presence of the fire, the earth, the air and water, I consecrate now this deck for now and ever.
Amen

Once the candle stops burning put all cards together and shuffle them twenty-two times. Wrap the deck in a brand new scarf or tablecloth and you are all set.

Performing a reading

It is important that your body and mind are clean to perform a reading. You can have a herbal bath with healing plants, for example rosemary, snake plant, petiveria, rue and sage or just rock salt. You should not be under the influence of alcohol or any other substance. Concentrate well, perform breathing exercises and focus on the reading. When you do any type of healing, reading, and/or working with people you must look after yourself very well. Many people search for a reading in moments of desperation, when they are experiencing fear or uncertainties and they often carry negative energy and spirits. Be prepared before reading for them.

The environment should be clean, as quiet as possible and always allocate a table where you perform the reading. Have crystals, plants, incenses and a candle. Some clairvoyants require the person to take the shoes off as ae sign of respect and grounding. Never perform a reading in your bedroom, close to the toilets, bars and public places, apart from festivals. Public places like bars have very mixed energies, often negative ones. If you are reading for other people you need to look after yourself, invoke your protection and detach from their energy. Have healing plants in the room, sage incense also helps. Do not use the same cards you use for yourself and do not read for anyone under the influence of drugs or alcohol.

Trust your intuition and your gut feelings to guide you to do everything you need to protect yourself, your environment and your wellbeing. You should be positive and welcoming but at the same time firm and confident. The most important thing is to orientate people, offer guidance, explain that a reading covers a maximum period of one year and remind them that their free will can change everything, regardless of what appears in the reading. Your main focus should always be on helping people. Only tell what you see in the cards and how your intuition interprets it, rather than giving your personal opinion and advice. It is important to be honest and if you see very negative cards, deliver the message in the most positive way you can. People often look for a reader to tell them what they want to hear. Be consistent and honest and inform the person you are reading for that the message you are delivering is based on what the cards are showing. Sometimes, adding your own personal advice becomes part of the misunderstanding, or disbelief.

Once you are proficient it is important that you charge something for a reading. If you don't need the money you can give it to charity. If you are reading for someone as a favour, you can charge the symbolic coin. In years of experience it is evidenced that people respect the reading more when they pay for it. Often people think that spiritual healers and clairvoyants should not charge. It is totally wrong, you do not charge for your spiritual gifts, you charge for your time as any other professional would. This also helps to balance the exchange of energy. Always value yourself, be assertive and confident; a good oracle reader doesn't use words like maybe, I think, or I don't know. Before closing off a reading, ask the person if they have any questions. If the querant does have further questions after you have completed the reading, let them know they are welcome to book another reading.

Increasing your Clairvoyance and Intuition

This subject can be very complex, some people are naturally aware of their clairvoyance from the time they are very young. Others discover in different stages of life that regardless of having a gift, they can increase and decrease clairvoyance during life. There are physical and mental aspects that help develop or enhance your intuition.

Physically, keep yourself hydrated, clean nutrition is important - avoid GMO food and chemicals. Soy has several toxins and can stimulate hormonal imbalance, which can affect your readings. Ensure that you sleep at least seven hours per night. Regular meditation is essential as well as daily prayer and gratitude affirmations. These will help align your energy and the spirits who surround you. It will be good for you anyway.

Apart from the basics above, there are exercises that will increase the control over your conscious and unconscious mind. Everyone has clairvoyance and intuition on different levels that permits the formulation and interpretation of specific signs. All you need is discipline and practice, which will dramatically improve your card reading.

Example 1
At night when you go to bed, visualize an object; build it in your mind and observe every single detail. If you lose the image go back and start again. Continue doing it until you fall asleep. You will find that after repeating this several times, the right side of your brain appears more alert. That means that you have a higher amount of blood in your brain.

In order to find your visual capacity it is necessary to be aware of feelings and physical changes in your body associated with certain situations or objects. In fact, there are spirits which work on regulating these physical changes and the most important thing is to ensure that your central nervous system and cognitive ability are intact. Observe every sign in your body when you are in different situations. It is scientifically proven that your gut is directly connected to your brain, hence you have a "gut feel". Start visualizing using geometric forms, first using a dot without a limit and later extend it into an endless line. Afterwards, you can create other lines, forms, designs and objects. You can visualize anything you want, notice what happens in your body with each visualization.

Example 2
Stand in front of a wall and use ear plugs to avoid any type of distraction. If you prefer, lay down and look at the ceiling. Try to visualize a house or another type of construction and include every possible little detail. Imagine entering from the front door and walking through the corridor into the lounge. You must feel the sensation of the floor under your feet. Walk towards each room in the building, touch the furniture, plants and decorations. Smell the scent in the air and pay attention to the materials used as much as possible. Try to recreate as many characteristics as possible in a concrete way. As you explore this property of your mind more and more, you will surprise yourself with the level of your sensorial perception and what you can build. It will bring to the surface a mixture of what your subconscious mind has already seen, not only in this life, but also in past lives.

Example 3
Sit comfortably and focus on the eye of your mind. Focus on someone you know very well. Try to visualize the entire person, every single detail, their individual style, the jewellery they wear, their lips, any markings they have, see their hands, nails, their eye colour and the colour and style of their hair. Remember the way this person moves their hands and eyes, gestures and their voice. Reach out and touch them on the hand and notice how they smell. Once all physical aspects are covered, focus on the person's thoughts, behaviours and feelings, cognition, opinions and personality. Finally, you will look into this person's spirituality. You can imagine someone you know, a friend, a family member or a deceased loved one. You will be impressed on how that person will appear in your dreams or even contact you soon.

Example 4
Camping is one of the best medicines ever! If you can, go camping somewhere close to water, near the ocean, by a river, waterfalls (these are the best), or even a bush bath. Have your feet in the ground and observe every detail of the plants and animals around you. It is better to observe wild animals rather than pets as they live their lives without human influence. Walk barefoot wherever you can and feel the ground under your feet. You will surprise yourself how these images will be recorded in your mind. This is how Gypsies found many symbols.

If you do these exercises regularly you will notice how your intuition will develop quickly and so will your clairvoyance. You also will feel better as a person because it all helps your mind to reach peace and balance.

Final Considerations

The Gypsy cards is a powerful oracle that combines several aspects of the symbols, numbers and suits. Many female clairvoyants decide not to read during their periods and if the moon is on third quarter. If you lack in confidence with the cards, don't hesitate to use the book to guide you, practice leads to mastery. Traditionally, only Romani men would read the cards, and this would be done during the day. However, today anyone can do it, any time of day or night. As long as you are prepared you can do it.

If a card falls to the ground before the spread is laid out, it carries a more important message than those of the spread. It is very important to interpret it well. If you find yourself feeling a bit low, or the person coming to you for a reading appears intoxicated or has a very negative energy, you are completely entitled to refuse service. If you deal a very negative spread, please stop the reading, perform a healing session and start again. Remember, you chose to read an oracle to improve your decision making, self-development and to help people, building positive karmic connections and empower whoever comes to you. Many blessings and live with passion.

Spreads

There are many reading methods, some are well known, others are not. Depending on intuition and practice, readers lay cards in different ways creating their own codes and feelings in relation to how they interpret the cards. Therefore, they can create their own methods of reading for each consultation, depending on what the question is and how long the reading will go for. Many aspects are important for each reading. Generally, a greater number of cards are used for broader questions. The more specific the question, the less cards required to determine the answers. The most important thing is to be prepared and follow your intuition and how you feel about the person consulting. Regardless of the method, be honest to the oracle and be helpful.

There are several different methods on the following pages. You can choose whichever spreads work best for you. All spreads are valid, but of course require practice and dedication. The more familiar you are with the cards the more natural your readings will become.

One Card – Yes/No

This is the ideal method if you need an answer to a closed question. It can also be utilised along with other spreads for specific aspects if the initial question was quite broad, and you want to pinpoint a straightforward answer.

Steps
1. Shuffle the cards at least three times, maximum seven, directing them to your heart.
2. Put the deck in the centre of the table.
3. Cut the deck into three separate piles.
4. Put the deck together in the order your intuition tells you (or the person consulting).
5. Open a "fan" with the design facing down.
6. Concentrate on the question and say it out loud.
7. Pick up one card with your left hand.

Interpretation
Interpret the card's meaning and the energy you feel. Look at how the card you have chosen can answer the question objectively. There are a few neutral cards in the deck. If you happen to choose one of these, take another card to determine the answer.

Card	Answer	Card	Answer
01 The Rider	Yes	19 The Tower	No
02 The Clover	No	20 The Garden	Yes
03 The Ship	Yes	21 The Mountain	No
04 The House	Yes	22 The Path	Yes
05 The Tree	Yes	23 The Rat	No
06 The Cloud	No	24 The Heart	Neutral
07 The Snake	No	25 The Ring	Yes
08 The Coffin	No	26 The Book	Yes
09 The Bouquet	Yes	27 The Letter	Neutral
10 The Sickle	No	28 The Gypsy Man	Yes
11 The Whip	Yes	29 The Gypsy Woman	Yes
12 The Birds	Yes	30 The Lily	Yes
13 The Child	Yes	31 The Sun	Yes
14 The Fox	No	32 The Moon	Neutral
15 The Bear	No	33 The Key	Yes
16 The Star	Yes	34 The Fish	Yes
17 The Stork	Yes	35 The Anchor	Yes
18 The Dog	Yes	36 The Cross	Yes

Two Card Spread

This spread works best for a specific question. It is important that you know the cards and their combinations well.

Steps
1. Shuffle the cards at least three times, maximum seven, directing them to your heart.
2. Put the deck in the centre of the table.
3. Cut the deck into three separate piles.
4. Put the deck together in the order your intuition tells you (or the person consulting).
5. Open a "fan" with the design facing down.
6. Concentrate on the question and say it out loud.
7. Pick up two cards with your left hand. It is very important to keep them in order as selected.

Interpretation
The reader must look at the card combination and consider what is relevant in the question.

Three Card Spread

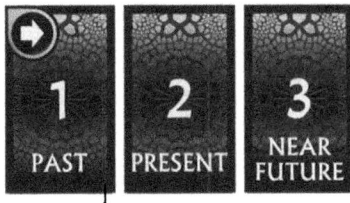

In this method the cards represent the time before the question, the time of the reading and the immediate future. However, your intuition can lead you to interpret it differently. It is extremely important to know the combinations to understand how to integrate the three into a solid answer

Steps
1. Shuffle the cards at least three times, maximum seven, directing them to your heart.
2. Put the deck in the centre of the table.
3. Cut the deck into three separate piles.
4. Put the deck together in the order your intuition tells you (or the person consulting).
5. Open a "fan" with the design facing down.
6. Concentrate on the question and say it out loud.
7. Pick up three cards with your left hand. It is very important to place them in the same order as depicted in the image above.

Interpretation
Traditionally it can be past, present and future, however using card combinations the reader can obtain a more detailed answer.

Five Card Spread – The Wheel of Fortune

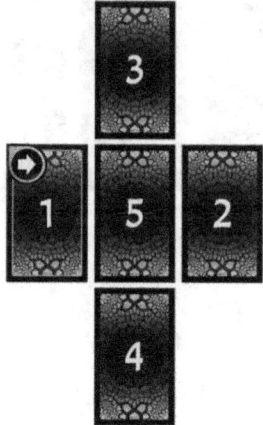

This spread offers a simple way to answer a specific question with relevant output in relation the chosen cards. Similar to the previous methods, you need to know the cards and how they can combine and interact.

Steps
1. Shuffle the cards at least three times, maximum seven, directing them to your heart.
2. Put the deck in the centre of the table.
3. Cut the deck into three separate piles.
4. Put the deck together in the order your intuition tells you (or the person consulting).
5. Open a "fan" with the design facing down.
6. Concentrate on the question and say it out loudly.
7. Pick up five cards with the left hand. Place them in the same order as depicted in the image above.

Interpretation
Card 1: Represents the current situation, the problem or the main question.
Card 2: Represents the influences of the past.
Card 3: Represents the energy towards near future.
Card 4: Represents what is hidden under the appearances.
Card 5: Represents the answer to the question and possible solution to the problem.

Celtic Cross

Each of the ten positions in this spread have traditional meanings that describe a specific area of life where certain influences and situations are happening, either internally or externally. This is a more complex spread and requires a certain level of proficiency.

Steps
1. Shuffle the cards at least three times, maximum seven, directing them to your heart.
2. Put the deck in the centre of the table.
3. Cut the deck into three separate piles.
4. Put the deck together in the order your intuition tells you (or the person consulting).
5. Open a "fan" with the design facing down.
6. Concentrate on the question whilst looking at the cards
7. Pick up ten cards with the left hand. It is very important to place them in the same order as depicted in the image above.

Interpretation

Card 1: This is the main card and it reflects the core of the situation of the querant.

Card 2: Called the crossed card, it describes what generates conflicts and barriers to the immediate present. It shows what blocks the path and indicates what is hindering the main card from expressing itself.

Card 3: The head card has a simple meaning since it is on top of the main card. It describes the environment and the situation that is in life now. It is what makes the meaning of the main card more evident.

Card 4: This is the base of the question and it describes the instincts, desires and the real reason that is reflected on the head card. The ground is where the root of the question is located. It helps you understand the contradiction of your dilemma.

Card 5: The influences of the past, something important that happened. The situation that comes before the main card becomes the centre. This is something that was important, but now has no significance apart from the lesson it provided.

Card 6: The influences of the future describes a situation that will manifest soon in the life of the querant. It is relevant to the immediate future only.

Card 7: The actual situation, this is an extension of the main card. It describes your attitude around the current circumstances. It reflects a combination of internal factors and your willingness to act and what is important to be developed.

Card 8: This card describes your environment and the perception family, friends and colleagues have about you regarding the current situation. It can reflect a phase in the individual's journey, and it can contradict your feelings.

Card 9: Fears and expectations. The anxieties and desires present in just this card.

Card 10: This card shows the outcome, the final answer to the main card. The word "final" is very subjective since the reading is relevant within the next six months and of course free will can alter any outcome.

The Gypsy Mandala Spread

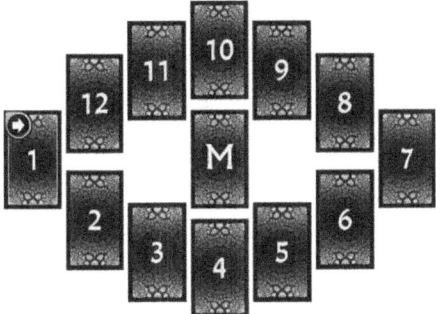

This spread is very efficient to perform a complex reading. Thirteen cards are used, the main (M) card and twelve others which are numbered sequentially are selected after the main card. The main card is placed in the centre of the table first and is only flipped once all other cards have been turned over. This method is often used by the Kallon clan.

Steps
1. Shuffle the cards at least three times, maximum seven, directing them to your heart.
2. Put the deck in the centre of the table.
3. Cut the deck into three separate piles.
4. Put the deck together in the order your intuition tells you (or the person consulting).
5. Open a "fan" with the design facing down.
6. Concentrate on the question whilst looking at the cards.
7. Choose your main card first with your left hand and place it face down in the centre of the table.
8. Select another twelve cards with your left hand. It is very important to place them in the same order as depicted in the image above.
9. Turn the cards over according to the order in the image with the main card being turned over last.

Interpretation
M Main Card to be placed in the centre. This is the most important overall focus of the reading.
Card 1: Aspects of the person, intentions and projects.

Card 2: Finances, earnings and expenses.
Card 3: Friends, family, short travel.
Card 4: Family, your origin and your roots.
Card 5: Pleasures, adventures, children and art.
Card 6: Profession, work and health.
Card 7: Partnerships, contracts, alliances and marriage.
Card 8: The hidden side of life, changes and transformations.
Card 9: Justice, bureaucracy and religion.
Card 10: Reputation, recognition and appearance to the world.
Card 11: Social life, network, projects and relationships.
Card 12: Hidden enemies, karmic inheritance.

The Gypsy Spread

1	2	3	4	5	6	7	8	9
10	11	12	13	14	15	16	17	18
19	20	21	22	23	24	25	26	27
28	29	30	31	32	33	34	35	36

This method is the most complex and efficient way to perform a reading. It does require an extensive understanding of the cards, knowledge of combinations and strong intuition. It is a lengthy reading and can take up to two hours. As you can see in the image above, all of the cards are used. This reading gives a strong view of your life or of the person consulting. By opening card by card, different chapters of a life story are told.

Steps
1. Shuffle the cards at least three times, maximum seven, directing them to your heart.
2. Put the deck in the centre of the table.
3. Cut the deck into three separate piles.
4. Put the deck together in the order your intuition tells you (or the person consulting).
5. Lay the cards in four lines of nine cards. It is very important to place them in the same order as depicted in the image above.

Interpretation

1	2	3	4	5	6	7	8	9
10	11	12	13	14	15	16	17	18
18	17	16	15	14	13	12	11	10
9	8	7	6	5	4	3	2	1

After laying all the cards as above, you should interpret them two by two. Flip the first card of the first line and the last card of the last line. Then read the second card of the first line with the second last card of the last line and so on until all the cards have been interpreted in the order depicted in the above image. Look into coherence in the symbols, descriptions, combinations and major and minor arcana using logic and intuition. This method is the most used by Romani people. It gives a general view of the present moment and indicates the influence of the future.

The Cards

Card	Page	Card	Page
01 The Rider	40	19 The Tower	93
02 The Clover	42	20 The Garden	96
03 The Ship	45	21 The Mountain	99
04 The House	48	22 The Path	102
05 The Tree	51	23 The Rat	105
06 The Clouds	54	24 The Heart	108
07 The Snake	57	25 The Ring	111
08 The Coffin	60	26 The Book	114
09 The Bouquet	63	27 The Letter	117
10 The Sickle	66	28 The Gypsy Man	120
11 The Whip	69	29 The Gypsy Woman	123
12 The Birds	72	30 The Lily	126
13 The Child	75	31 The Sun	129
14 The Fox	78	32 The Moon	132
15 The Bear	81	33 The Key	135
16 The Star	84	34 The Fish	138
17 The Stork	87	35 The Anchor	141
18 The Dog	90	36 The Cross	144

Card 01 - The Rider

Element ~ Fire

In this card we can see a rider. A courageous and humble gypsy man on his horse with knowledge and mastery, he is looking for something, or searching for his own destiny. He is confident and determined. The gypsy rider is a man who likes having his shirt open, showing his heart and feeling the wind. His horse shows that his mission is peaceful, and his protection is divine.

Major Arcana
The Rider is in a hurry to accomplish and achieve his goals. He trusts himself and has initiative in his actions. Note that the man is not being taken by a charioteer, it is he who drives his horse – he is in charge.

Minor Arcana
The Nine of Hearts is one of the best cards in the deck and brings a period of many joys and satisfactions. It is the representation of joy for conquering desires. And joy attracts more luck.

Interaction between the arcana
The arrival of a novelty with joys, bringing personal and collective growth. Often this novelty is brought by someone. However, depending on the position in which the card comes out, it often also asks us to be bolder and not limit our opportunities. It's time to take hold of the reins of life and move on.

Positive Aspects
You will be full of boldness and courage; you will gain a lot of wisdom on your journey. The Rider card indicates that the conquest is near, and you have everything needed to reach it. Just believe in your senses and give value to your projects. Do not let anyone delay you or try to hold you back. Soon you will cross the finish line and be victorious. There is nothing more pleasant than being able to see your dreams come true.

Negative Aspects
When this card is surrounded by negative cards in a spread, it means that various obstacles will come your way. It will not be easy to reach your goal. Life and treacherous people will try to stop you. As complicated as it may seem, do not waste time looking for escapes, jump over hurdles and move on. If you have planted only good things in this life, only good things you can reap. Never forget the Law of Attraction, everything that goes, returns.

Work and Finances
If you're looking for work, the Rider indicates that you will soon be employed, probably via assistance from a friend. However, do not stand still and wait; go after what you want! Now is a good time to reap what you planted. You should conduct business with more boldness, firmness and belief in your goals. It takes attitude, get out of the comfort zone or laziness so that your goals are achieved. If you are bold, you will soon have much prosperity.

Love and Relationship
Singles: Soon someone important and special will come, who will bring happiness and the possibility of a solid future.

In a Relationship: If you want something concrete such as a wedding proposal, an official status, a recognition of the relationship or children, this moment is perfect for that with great vibes full of blessings.

General Aspects
New beginnings, resets, spirituality, action, creativity, seduction and willpower. New projects, new mission, new job, wisdom to resolve problems quickly and concrete ideas. It can mean self-discovery, something is on your way, explore your talents, find a hobby or a new profession.

Message
Success, prosperity, good luck and reward.

Card 02 - The Clover

Element ~ Air

The Clover is the opposition of card one, The Rider. In card 2, The Rider finds the Clover on the way. This card is described in some decks as scattered stones and wood, the first obstacles. It is also known as the Clover of Luck, symbolizing that in the pursuit of happiness, we are counting on luck and suggesting that at the end of the story we will get what we desire. We are often responsible for our own lack of structure and therefore depending on fears and favours.

Major Arcana

On one hand two means divergence, struggle or conflict, on the other it means union and cooperation. The Clover represents luck, and the colour green depicts protection. Within the project initiated by the Rider it is necessary to realize which path is heading to contentment and where it is necessary to adapt to reality. It may be necessary to circumvent your destination and the barriers in order to perfect the project and your own performance. The Clover denotes a time of redirection.

Minor Arcana

The Six of Diamonds is a card of generosity and exchange. It offers what is good and receives also. It suggests help and reward, although do not count on it. Humility is necessary to recognize you need help. Receptivity: in times of difficulty be generous towards others. At the height of a crisis, luck often appears. In that sense, it's like a resistance test. Just have firmness of purpose and decision. This card suggests this is a time of personal improvement and adjustment within circumstances. Some difficult situations must be overcome. You may be receiving the benevolence of life and people in greater quantity than you provide. There are new opportunities to choose when you realize your possibilities, and you do not stop in front of a path. When a person is ready to share what is good with those who have less, they reap good results.

Interaction between the Arcana

After we have done everything we can, overcame challenges, learned from The Clover and improved our projects and performance, it is time to continue a great journey. Let's leave behind some things and go into the unknown. Not everything can be controlled or predicted.

Positive Aspects

Focus on what you want, The Clover asks you to set your goals with love. Let them be your source of energy because everything that is probation will surely pass. This will be a phase where you'll add a lot of self-knowledge, become a more mature person and a source of inspiration for many people. This is where the obstacles represented by this card will test you to see if you are determined enough to deserve what you dream to achieve. Do not forget good friends, they will be great company at this stage. Stop, reflect and ask yourself: how much is my happiness worth? Am I heading in the right direction? You already know that being happy is priceless, so go ahead and show everyone that your passage here is not a game, and that you are sure of your value and know you deserve to achieve your goals.

Negative Aspects

It will be a difficult but transient period. It's time to prove the magnitude of your faith and determination, the kind of difficulty you'll face is associated with the other cards that come out with The Clover in the spread. This is likely to be a difficult period for a short time, there are sticks and stones in the way. Constraints: The Clover does not indicate any type of permanent loss. It hinders but does not stop. Transposable difficulties, you must fight to overcome the obstacles, and in this way, you will surely get what you want.

Work and Finances

Beware of gossip and stay away from conflicts, this is not the time to speak up. Avoid acting without being sure of your safety, tread carefully, do not be too eager and rush into anything. If you are unemployed, The Clover warns you that it is really a complicated phase but suggests you don't lose focus as it is fleeting, and you are able to overcome the obstacles. The Clover warns us that unforeseen trials and barriers may appear. This is a time where you will see the extent of your will to win. Only those who recognize their true worth know that there is no difficulty they can't surmount in their quest for a complete and happy life. Projects, plans and proposals should be reassessed, reoriented, and redirected, adapting theories to reality and practical circumstances. There is a test of reality and consistency of goals. You may give up realizing that you did not want to overcome challenges even if you could.

Love and Relationship

Single: Your spirit is still surrounded by uncertainties because of past relationships. Be strong and never stop, continue your journey with great faith and open your heart to happiness.

In a Relationship: The Clover in Love also represents complicated times. There will be uncertainties surrounding the relationship. This is a phase that calls for conversation, patience and understanding. Analyse everything before assuming the worst. Do not take steps longer than your legs, believe in love if it stays alive, and above all only point out defects and problems that really need to be corrected for the benefit of the couple. This is not the time to make risky conclusions.

General Aspects

Learning, maturity, insecurity, crisis, dislikes, obstacles, arguments, disagreements, negativity, difficulty, momentary problems that we must overcome. The Clover reminds us of the need to rely on our inner strength and tells us to take a moment to reflect before making decisions. What works is a test of the firmness of purpose, ability and self-confidence. Going beyond card 2 is to grow. Seek guidance from another person if necessary, it can be from a friend or someone who knows the situation you are dealing with. It is necessary to be willing to recognize failures; to learn, to exchange, to challenge oneself and through this process of maturing, to grow. Internally it is the person himself who is creating obstacles because of insecurity and negative thoughts that nourish blocks, limitations, lack of concrete views, doubt, fear, discouragement, hesitation, anger, depression and prejudice. Externally they are obstacles placed by other people or circumstantial difficulties depending on the environment and what the situation involves.

Message

The lucky clover symbolizes the action of providence, a new opportunity.

Card 03 - The Ship

Element ~ Water

The Ship is the messenger in our journey that we walk between life and death. One sees the sea and a great ship. Don't be frightened, this card only wants to indicate positive changes that will occur in your life with wisdom, self-knowledge and growth. They can come from yourself or some external event that will happen soon. Your request is to allow yourself to live new emotions, to discover new desires and curiosities, because the world is huge and full of things you don't yet know along with possibilities that can add much value to your life.

The sea is calm, and you are safe in this journey. See possible new horizons that even if they bring uncertainty, will give a rejuvenated energy in your spirit and that pleasant sensation of not being anchored. The worst thing that exists is when we think there is nothing more to enjoy or discover in this life. So, embark on this trip with no regrets, without clinging to the past and without delaying the actions for yourself to be happy. This is the greatest gift you can give to yourself.

In health the card asks for attention with fluid retention, blood pressure and kidneys.

Major Arcana
The Ship represents a journey, a change or end of a cycle. The change will be radical, but not to be afraid of because it will be beneficial.

Minor Arcana
The Ten of Spades represents the end of a phase. Despite the pain, it's time to get up and look for another path.

Interaction between the Arcana
Changes are on the way. They will be radical and there may be pain but they will be beneficial and transformative. It is like a journey in a rough sea, but it will lead to a dry land. The challenge will be inevitable. The Ship represents moments of great stress, fatigue or discouragement which must be overcome. You must rest or do activities that please you.

Positive Aspects
This is a positive card which indicates happy times and new territories to discover. You will be in spiritual peace and the doors of life will open for you. Rely on your creativity to make everything more interesting and relaxing. If you have an opportunity to travel then invest in this idea, it will be rewarding for your soul. What you live now can change the whole path of your life, so plant good times and look for happiness to grow. Know that your future will be much more interesting.

Negative Aspects
The journey of life must be lived wisely and patiently, so do not be in a hurry to make things happen. The negative side of this card only manifests when there is recklessness - you can miss good opportunities, let interesting moments pass by or spoil a project that would have everything to succeed if it was well crafted.

Work and Finance
The Ship suggests a good financial situation, with repayment of old debts and stability. For work this card depends very much on other cards drawn overall, but it is important to remember that its main message is the one of change. If you own a business, you will see good opportunities arise, perhaps in the form of a partnership. If you're employed, it is likely that a better proposal will appear, it may be within the current company or a new job offer. If you're unemployed, the tide of chance will be behind you, changes in your life will emerge and you will be prepared for this new step. The Ship indicates a process of life changes that will affect the whole routine to which you are accustomed, but understand your message as positive, a sea of good energies that will take you to the best destination. This card brings the message of the possibility of promotion and

financial improvement; however, with more challenges and responsibilities. It is possible that an opportunity will arise in another city or country.

Love and Relationship

Single: This is a good time to take a trip and relax. You will soon meet a person who will transform your life, and there is a possibility of marriage or a long-term commitment within a short time. It will be a relationship different from all previous ones. It is likely to be someone from another town or country.

In a Relationship: This card shows a moment with a little instability, so be patient. Know how to love and listen, soon this bad tide will pass. If the only way out is to end the relationship, simply accept it because destiny has new moments of love ahead in store for you. Have self-control, do not hide too much, love is a flower that is cultivated slowly. This card recommends a trip to increase the intimacy of the couple. If you are currently separated, The Ship indicates the end of the relationship. If Gypsy Man, Gypsy Woman or Rider cards are close by, they represent the arrival of another person.

General Aspects

Change, affection, sensitivity, new horizons, kindness, happiness, self-control and the search for balance. The spiritual and unconscious world. The movement of new and powerful energies of wellbeing. Great adventure. Here the changes are slow, but lasting and stable. Surprises will come as rewards of life and commitment employed in the past. Promising future, sincerity, honesty, progress, achievement, loyalty. Distant places, foreign lands. The Ship can also represent the correction of aspects of the past and a change of direction in life.

Message

Changes, travel and adventures.

Card 04 - The House

Element ~ Earth

The House is card number 4 of the Gypsy Deck and it is positive. You are a disciplined person, and this will take you on the path of achievements. It symbolizes the union between heaven and earth. This card represents our foundations in life; it can be work and all kinds of relationships. Its image is a safe place, something we know and trust. Although we have ups and downs in life, there is nothing better than our home to feel welcomed and protected. The House also represents the emotional protection we need to succeed in our plans.

Remember that your body is also a temple, the dwelling of your soul, so The House also symbolizes its interior and exterior, its structure. You will find much of your strength in family members. They motivate you and make you want to win, they are like your fuel. After all, it is not fun to live for ourselves if we do not share our glories and achievements with the loved ones.

Major Arcana
The House represents security, balance and effective protection we need to act in the world and succeed. Our homes are where we experience most of the ups and downs of daily life. Psychologically, the exterior of the house is the mask or appearance of a human being, the roof is the head and the spirit, the control of consciousness; the lower floors mark the level of the unconscious and the instincts; the kitchen is the place of psychic transmutations or inner evolution.

Minor Arcana

The figure of the King of Hearts represents the maximum achievement of the domain to which the question refers. Being the supreme figure of authority, he represents someone with power, maturity, knowledge gained through experience, and wisdom that makes others often come for his advice. In a reading, he quite often represents the husband, father or someone for whom you have a deep affection. He is always a man of some age, with a heart of gold, who has reached the highest level in the sentimental domain.

Interaction between the Arcana

The King of Hearts usually symbolizes the father. In this protective and loving figure is a man who values the sentimental side and cherishes his family. This card can also represent the neighbourhood, what is around your house can be seen by the cards next to it. Health wise, this card calls attention to your blood pressure and heart. You are a good company and a great advisor to others, but do not forget to listen to advice from the ones who love you.

Positive Aspects

Now is the moment to share time with the family, to be with those you love and to accept the advice and care of those who know you best. Your spirit will be in a strong phase and the good energies will nourish your soul by encouraging you and leading you to the best answers and possible roads. Do not forget that you are also a part of this world and your loved ones count on your support too; your advice will be very well accepted and heard.

Negative Aspects

Do not ignore family conflicts or the needs of your spirit. You need to find your balance point and create your outer structure. You will need to gain self-knowledge, meditate and look deep within you to find a resolution. Don't be afraid, when you are in harmony you'll be able to be a great influence for the loved ones who live in your home. Remember, you are also a key player in the lives of those around you. The House can also represent a comfort zone that leaves you stuck, hindering your evolution.

Work and Finances

The House reflects a time of success, all your choices are right and your wise way will help you achieve your goals. Believe in your potential and value your closest friends in your workplace, they will be the key contributors to your recognition. If you are unemployed use the good energy of this card to chase after the job you are looking for. You will find it, have faith! The House card shows the home of your soul and all who dwell in your love and consideration; loved ones, those who influence your life and are part of your daily decisions. It symbolizes the place you reach at the end of the day, to rest, find shelter and protection. It also signifies financial stability.

Love and Relationship

Single: Someone will bring a feeling of warmth to your heart. Count on the friendliest people to open your heart. Someone new may surprise you and become a part of your home. A new love whom you can trust.

In a Relationship: This is the time to retreat into the arms of your loved one and enjoy an affectionate phase where you will be able to complete one another. There will be no obstacles that you wouldn't be able to overcome if you take notice of communication and feelings that involve them.

General Aspects

Balance, structure, security, family matters, stability, trust and affective support. Moral values, inflexibility, resistance to change. Proclamation of prosperity, success in ventures, happiness and favourable investments. Work, organization, progress, material gains, power and realization. In this card we find, above all, the necessity of organizing and structuring our lives in the emotional and interior fields which often become unbalanced with daily worries. The House also represents daily life, practicalities, the constant balance that we should seek to live better. It can represent our home or someone's house, or the people next to us.

Message

It's a message of favour, blessings in many ways and balance. Security and protection.

Card 05 - The Tree

Element ~ Earth

Card 5 of the Gypsy Deck is The Tree. With its roots pinning it to the ground, it gives us feelings of security and stability. The representation is associated with the group and the family spirit because it is in this environment that we learn to grow and transmit our culture, beliefs and learning. Through the Tree we receive the aspect of strong connection to traditions passed down for generations which may prevent us from evolving and understanding the diversities of this Universe. Due to the duality of possibilities with The Tree, its meaning is established with greater clarity taking into account the other cards that accompany it. In one reading, it can mean a safe harbor, in another The Tree may want to warn you about changes needed so that you can effectively balance the knowledge of the old with the excitement of the new.

Major Arcana
The Tree with its roots planted firmly on the ground reminds us of the feeling of stability and expansion. It is a card that represents family, relationships, closed groups such as clans where there is protection of values that are passed down from generation to generation. A person represented by the tree has strong traditions or follows standards by pure convention, and perhaps should question this.

Minor Arcana

The Seven of Hearts can represent the arrival of someone or the establishment or resumption of harmonious relations between two people. This card also reflects the personal consciousness of "me". All actions taken so far will contribute to the consolidation of this image. However, you need to check if your internal standards should be changed in order to achieve your new goals.

Interaction between the Arcana

The Tree card can speak of both security and about changes and reflections on the old patterns. Although the teachings passed from generation to generation have been assimilated and applied in a positive way, one must look for the balance between the new and the old, bringing a version that suits this life. When this happens, there will be a harvest of what has been planted, and the enterprises in which it is invested will be profitable. Thus, the person will feel more comfortable to share its fruits. In either sense, always think of the deep and stable roots of an ancient tree. Check which of these aspects fits your question. If it is related to another question, interpret according to the meaning of the card. Also check the other cards in the spread to get a better picture of your answer.

Positive Aspects

You will see all of your effort and investment bear fruit. After all the waiting and the battle to get where you are now, you will finally find the signal you need to know you are on the right path. For this to occur, it is necessary that you allow the new to be part of your life without forgetting the knowledge you have acquired so far on your journey. You will now be able to apply it in the wisest way possible. Now is the time to feel fulfilled and share this happiness with your loved ones.

Negative Aspects

Depending on the cards that come with it, The Tree can alert you to something that is holding you to old beliefs and outdated thoughts. Your stubbornness in not understanding the new will imprison you in a world that although seems safe, prevents you from finding the true achievements This poses a huge barrier in the need to move forward and evolve with new learning.

Work and Finances
You seek stability in the professional world. If you are working, know that your commitment will be recognized and you will reap the fruits of recognition soon. If you have your own business, be very careful about too many illusions or plans, the chances of progress are very high so be sure that you would gain something from your efforts. If you are unemployed, it was probably by choice, so structure your way forward in the way you want to go. Use your willpower to set you in the direction you want to travel. The Tree brings with it great promises of achievement because you have sown your dreams for life and in return it will bring you the fruits, so enjoy the moment of harvest! In relation to finance, it is unlikely that you are someone who invests or lends without guarantees. You are more likely to be someone who likes to pay cash to ensure you have no financial problems. However, there is a possibility of unexpected expenses in relation to housing or mobile assets which may bring challenges.

Love and Relationship
Single: There is someone coming your way who is likely to propose you an old-fashioned courtship, with dating, engagement and marriage. This person likes to make sure everything is just right down to the smallest detail as tradition dictates.

In a Relationship: You are in a stable and transparent moment in the relationship, so you already know that there are some customs that are unlikely to change over time, learn to accept them. You have the necessary synergy for both of you to have a lasting and fulfilled relationship. Do not forget to take some time out of the routine to enjoy yourselves more.

General Aspects
Sharing, fraternity, maturity, stability, rebirth, life, need for giving and receiving, fair and loyal exchanges. Detachment, selflessness, altruism and unconditional giving. Good health and healing. The need to share what is gained, for happiness must be for all at the same time. Create roots. A birth or a proposition is eminent. The Universe is conspiring positively, reap what you planted. Maturity and family ties. Bounty, gains, harvest, wealth, prosperity, triumph and joy. The power of achievement with solidity.

Message
Solid family and relationships.

Card 6 - The Clouds

Element ~ Air

The Clouds card has a celestial energy and is sometimes called "The Winds" in other decks. This card represents instability (after all, clouds change shape all the time), so according to its meaning it can bring rain that can either hydrate or destroy. In the Gypsy Deck this card has the image of heavy clouds that cover most of the sky, hiding the sunlight. It symbolizes difficulty in making decisions because many things cannot be seen and indicates that the mind is tumultuous and confused.

Major Arcana
The Clouds advise you that this is not a good time to make decisions or act. It is wise to wait for the sun to rise again, wait for the storm to pass and see how everything looks differently then. It would pay off to be cautious and patient at this time. Remain steady as the Clouds pass through Heaven, thus avoiding greater damage, caused by you. This card depicts a time when everything seems confusing and gloomy and suggests this is not a good time to evaluate or judge situations even if there are new opportunities in your life; wait until everything becomes clearer. The Clouds generally indicate more about mental and emotional situations than about the material and physical. This card may also indicate development of a spiritual gift that needs to be worked on.

Minor Arcana

The King of Clubs represents the energy of pure fire. He is not interested in creativity or dreaming up ideas and implementing them himself. Instead, he is more inclined to have an idea and change the world to match his vision. As such, he is a born leader of all kinds of people, and he is a great visionary. Once he sets himself a goal, he adheres to it and ensures that he can make it happen with the support of those around him. People naturally gravitate around this King as they know he will get things done and get them done very well. He is a master at getting other people to do the work for him and manages to keep them on the side throughout the process.

Interaction between the Arcana

The King of Clubs can indicate a mature but troubled man who is undecided. Do not despair, in the darkest afflictions, remember that it is from the black clouds that crystal clear water comes. It is a call to face uncertainties, doubts and confusion of feelings in the face of the challenges (clouds) of life. These can be solved by letting the inner warrior act, facing the issues and using all the will power of the King of Clubs

Positive Aspects

When this card appears in a reading, The Clouds usually pass quickly which means that this turbulent period will soon be over. The best news is that the new opportunities will soon arise after their passage, so it is best to wait for good winds to come and blow The Clouds away. Life is always full of challenges and surprises; we must use these moments as an opportunity for learning and growth. There is a reason for everything that comes into your life, try to absorb the best way to understand the lesson and possibilities that can come from this confusing passage. Reflect on everything that happens and try not to make decisions during this phase. Study the paths and as soon as The Clouds pass, you will easily see the exit.

Negative Aspects

The mind will be a mess, so it is best not to make any decisions at this time. Uncertainties will take over your life and nothing will seem very clear. You will possibly go through a time filled with doubts and contradictory ideas, nothing is too cohesive, and it seems that there is no safe way out of trouble. It is best to wait for the clouds to pass, to guard your thoughts and take care with decisions.

Work and Finances
This card is related to your mental and physical health. Therefore, this entire storm is the way you will see current situations. It seems that nothing is cleared easily and that everything conspires against you. However, it is not always that way. If you are unemployed it will be a difficult time to do interviews; if they do appear, stay as confident as possible. If you are employed and are in a complicated situation, do not take risks. Do not choose an offensive stance or make rush decisions. You will be easily irritated and solutions will not be clear to you. This is not a good time to take the lead on important matters. If you are an entrepreneur, do not do anything risky, let things follow their routine flow for now, is not an advisable moment for important decisions. The Clouds just wants to give you a message: Wait! It is time to reflect, to calm down. This moment is fleeting, soon these charged clouds will move on and the Sun will appear for you.

Love and Relationship
Single: This card represents the present. In the Gypsy Deck, the clouds are very heavy, which means moments of doubt to start a relationship. It's best not to jump to conclusions, expect this period of heavy energy to pass. Accept it is not the time and believe that many good things will come as soon as it is over.

In a Relationship: Focus on the idea that every relationship has its ups and downs, so it's no use feeding the problems knowing that this is not the right time. Even if you are desperate for a resolution that you cannot see, do not be afraid right now. The answers are not obvious but will become clear as soon as the clouds disappear. It is the time when you can gauge how strong your relationship is and just how powerful you are to overcome barriers together.

General Aspects
Doubt, moment of indecision, confusion, internal conflicts and unstable situations. Ease of creating problems, overreacting and lack of clarity. The material and physical problems can interfere with the emotional and spiritual area. In one interpretation, this card is not generally seen as final but transitory. Though alarmingly negative it is extremely important for inner growth and maturity. It indicates anxiety and health problems which may be caused by mental aspects, negative beliefs and transient turbulence. But it is an opportunity for purification and cleansing.

Message
Time out, patience and wait.

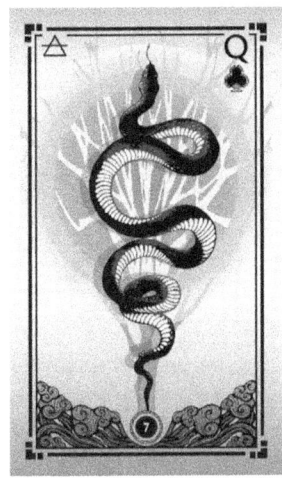

Card 7 - The Snake

Element ~ Air

The Snake is the number 7 card in the Gypsy Deck. Its meaning is not as negative as people usually think. The reason is simple. Imagine a serpent in a forest - if she comes to attack you at no time she is in an act of betrayal, in fact she defends herself from you who poses a threat. Therefore, the snake does not indicate betrayal as most people think, if it appears in a spread it doesn't mean people are plotting against you. It does mean you must be careful with the steps you take in your life. This is not to say you should stop taking risks and moving forward, but you should pay attention to the things you do and act in a cohesive and safe way. Be wise and patient. Now is not the best time for you to try and solve situations around you, this can put you in a boring or even complicated place. So, pay close attention to outcomes and seize opportunities to clarify and resolve outstanding issues without leaving unresolved baggage.

In health this card asks you to be attentive when you are feeling agitated. Look for relaxing activities to mitigate the negative charge you currently may have. It can also symbolize gynaecological and urological problems, stay tuned to your body.

Major Arcana

Hardly anyone imagines that a snake is good news, but in fact she asks us for care and attention. Many associate their symbolic sense with betrayal, but as we think of the animal, the card tells us that something may be lurking. If you walk in a forest, you know you can find snakes. Take care to remember that you are in their environment. The snakes are not hidden there waiting to attack you, therefore there is no betrayal. But if you present any threat to them they will not reflect before attacking you. Therefore, when walking in the forest be alert and prepared.

Minor Arcana
The Queen of Clubs represents a very determined woman in everything she does, a great director, especially for things related to work and money.

Interaction between the Arcana
This card is challenging, but it does give us some advice: be wise and do not challenge the snake. Be aware of what is happening around you. It does not mean that things will necessarily go wrong. We must act with more awareness and less innocence.

Positive Aspects
The snake comes with the warning that you must be careful where you step, be wise, do not rush, calm down, and analyse. Watch your back on everything that is happening around you. This card is not a sign that bad things will happen, you just need to be smart enough to stay safe and wise enough to know that everything has its right time and don't act recklessly.

Negative Aspects
You may be very agitated, and this energy can lead you to the worst possible path. Your lack of focus can hurt you by making you stressed. The rush will only lead you to bad answers and the lack of prudence will leave you in complicated situations.

Work and Finances
In this aspect you need to be extremely cautious and aware to avoid creating the worst possible outcome. Avoid talking about co-workers and your personal life at work. You may be opening yourself up too much to the wrong people, so avoid parallel conversations at work as this may land you in unpleasant situations. If you are feeling pressured by your workload, act calm and strive for balance. If you are unemployed do not throw yourself at any job opportunity that appears as it may leave you disappointed. Pay attention to how you behave during interviews, you may come across as desperate and say the wrong things. The snake appears in the spread as a warning card that asks you to be careful with the path you are following and the possible pitfalls you can come across.

In finance, be persistent and work hard so that the situation can improve. Beware of unnecessary expenses.

Love and Relationship

Single: Beware of this current energy because your recent relationships are likely to have been just sexual. However, it is not the fault of the person you involved yourself with, but yours. In an explosion of emotions, you surrender and then find yourself lost, not knowing what to do next. If you are looking for something more serious then focus on what it takes to really find a person who completes you.

In a Relationship: If you are in a relationship and it doesn't seem to be going well, now is not the best time to end it. Your impulsiveness can cause you to make a bad decision, and once you've acted, you may regret it. Think calmly and carefully about what you expect and want from your life and whether that relationship is keeping you from following this path or does not add anything of value for you.

General Aspects

Distress, falsehood, dishonesty, gossip, aggression, anger, hatred, intrigues, arguments, unfair losses, de-structuring, fights, bad characters crossing your path, conflicts and disagreements. Self-sabotage, treachery of oneself, do not allow yourself to be poisoned. Usually the dangers announced by this card are premeditated, planned and aware. Someone is likely to come into your life to disturb. Fragile health and problems that always come and go. Beware of infections, unprotected sex and substance abuse. It advises to use intelligence and mental acumen to attain wisdom and to guard against many dangers, new and ongoing. Stay sober, if you have an addiction, seek immediate help. It is not a positive warning at any time, especially for material and love matters. Guard yourself against negative external energies. Have the courage to face a situation of revealed danger. Defend your goals. It can also bring the message that we need to acknowledge and transform our inner darkness to strengthen personal power.

Message

Logical thinking, sobriety, strategy and calmness are necessary.

Card 8 - The Coffin

Element ~ Fire

If this card has appeared in your spread, there is no need to get tense. Card 8 of the Gypsy Deck, The Coffin is not always synonymous with death, but the energy of transition, do not forget that death is only a passage towards a fresh start; with any ending comes a new beginning. This card has neutral representation and symbolizes the justice of the conclusion. The Coffin advises a search along the spiritual path, not out of weakness but for the preparation of your "me" to receive a rebirth openly. Abandon everything that binds you to the past, bad times were teachings that made you a stronger person; the good times are there to fill your heart with hope, and to make you believe that it is possible to see flowers even after long storms. Whatever bad times have happened, now there will be light on your chest and no shackles on your feet.

When we talk about health, The Coffin asks you to pay more attention to your blood, especially sugar. Maybe it's time for a routine check-up.

Major Arcana
Contrary to what it seems, this card means transformation, rebirth. It indicates the end of one cycle and the beginning of another. This is a positive indication as it announces spiritual help for the realization of plans and projects. This card carries with it the sign of a cycle that has kept us from exploring new paths and finding new alternatives, the energy that incites the search for spiritual development. Nothing is forever, we are not eternal. And so all phases of our lives should be, and we should with the same happiness receive the good

vibrations and bid farewell to what has been completed. It is a sign of wisdom, growth, and good use of this time of life.

Minor Arcana
This influence brings confidence and encouragement typical of the Nine of Diamonds. Perhaps daring to try is better than failing to do so. Practical issues will be better addressed directly. Financial security can be expected as life resumes with good omens. Courage and honesty are the key words of this card. Spiritual forces will work for you if there is inner stability and strength of purpose.

Interaction between the Arcana
It is up to you to learn to deal with the events that this card of the Gypsy Deck indicates. It is important to take advantage of all situations that happen in life, even the negative. For all situations, there is a teaching and foundation behind them. Therefore, a phase that results in pain and suffering can serve as a force to overcome certain events. At the same time this card represents a new chapter of life, indicating that there are phases of life that will now be left behind. Now is the moment of rebirth and especially renewal. This card indicates that it is necessary to leave behind old habits and routines, whether in the physical, emotional or psychological world, to start a new chapter. As the life cycle requires, it is time to finalize one phase to start another. This card can also indicate a favourable moment for negative energies that call for and demand changes in attitudes, even more so if the Snake and Candle cards appear with The Coffin.

Positive Aspects
Once again, your life resumes. Projects and setbacks have been completed and we must see with the same eyes as the Gypsies, the prospect of happiness in the unknown. Encourage yourself, there is nothing to fear as long as you believe in your ability, walk with integrity and remain loyal to your principles. Moving on is a great natural gift of existing. Keep faith by feeding your spirit, wisdom to your mind and willpower to your physical body and you will see that you are able to achieve more than you imagined by not limiting yourself to a world spent.

Negative Aspects
Negative changes may occur. The Coffin can indicate obstacles, however, other cards with negative energy need to be present to induce this. Proceed with caution and review the last steps you have taken and you're likely to find an

error on this path. Face challenges that arise and do not be intimidated. Everyone makes mistakes, this only makes you more human, with greater possibilities to understand life better.

Work and Finances
Now is the time to take advantage of any signs of good opportunities that arise, regardless of your employment status. This card can indicate positive changes in workplace or business. Be aware of the signs the Universe is sending you and remain dedicated to what you believe to be of value to your life. If you are unemployed, do not be discouraged. Believe that soon your path will change for the better; the more you are worried and tense, the more it will show on your face, so you will not get the credibility you deserve in interviews. The Coffin is nothing more than the expression of resumption, renewal and the opportunity of new meetings and achievements. Fill your heart with the will to live and follow the good winds to achieve success.

Love and Relationship
Single: Forgetting the illusions you have experienced will help you to see the true beauty in yourself and will make it easier for others to see it too. Be wise, the world will send you new opportunities for passion and romance - do not waste time looking back.

In a Relationship: Detachment from the energies of the past. You have a story and it must be nurtured with something new, this is a way of maturing for both of you. Transformations will emerge in your relationship. This card may indicate a breakthrough for something more serious, like arrival of a child.

General Aspects
Radical change, something that has lost its life or importance. It can be either material or spiritual losses, terminations, disruptions, separations, the end of a cycle at the beginning of another. The changes that need some necessary and inevitable ends. A difficult phase that is over and time to move forward for a continuous evolution. It's the putrefaction of all that is old, unnecessary and futile for inner growth. In life everything is conceived, born, lives, matures and dies to be reborn, thus passing through all processes of transmutation. It does not represent physical death, or death with a tragic end, but with means for rebirth.

Message
Transformations and growth.

Card 9 - The Bouquet

Element ~ Air and Earth infusion

Card 9 of the Gypsy Deck, The Bouquet brings the message of much love for life, being of any kind, familiar to you, or between the loved ones that surrounds you.

A bouquet of flowers has several meanings, the difference is in the types of flowers. Each flower carries a different symbol, but all establish the message of affection and strong connection of the giver with the recipient. This card suggests that you will spend moments of deep happiness so intensely that you will not know how to control it, and the smile on your face will follow you for many days. Your positive energy will only bring more good things into your life and you will find yourself achieving various goals and dreams. Your aura will also brighten everyone closer to you, allowing you to have beautiful moments together.

Watch out for stress and emotional health. Sometimes being too rational can have bad consequences. Relax a bit, do some dancing, yoga, physical activities or something that gives you pleasure.

Major Arcana
We usually present a bouquet of flowers to people we love. Of course, receiving a bouquet is always lovely; as well as receiving something beautiful, we get this feeling of gratitude and the care and affection of the giver. The Bouquet

represents love, understanding between people, generosity, the gift or recognition of a victory.

Minor Arcana

The Queen of Spades is a very rational and determined woman, sometimes even domineering. She is an independent woman who rolls up her sleeves. Do not rest until you have achieved your goals, especially those linked to materiality, work or money.

Interaction between the Arcana

This card tells that you will receive many good gifts. Depending on how you deal with your current project or issue, if everything is well planned, you will have the satisfaction of accomplishing your goals. One piece of advice from this card is to reflect on the challenges you face in setting goals and fighting for them. In the end, expect to be crowned with laurels, or rather, you will receive your Bouquet.

Positive Aspects

This is probably one of the most positive cards in the Gypsy Deck. The bouquet indicates a moment of happiness, fulfilment and full joy. Your spiritual side will also be overflowing with good energies and will guide you through the best paths and choices. Good relationships will be established at this stage, and those who were already close, will be even closer to you. Good friendships will be a big help, because you will also be a great counsellor and friend to them. Seize this moment for greater self-knowledge, enrich your soul even more, fill your heart with flowers and good promises.

Negative Aspects

With so much love around you, you can become a little jealous and obsessive. You do not need to lock people who love you by your side; they will always come back because you are already enlightened and do them well. Do not let these heavy feelings that limit our lives take hold of your heart at this delicate and loving stage.

Work and Finances

The Bouquet also brings moments of accomplishment to the professional area. This is the time when you will receive your laurels for all your dedication. Many profits will come your way, and if you are unemployed, rejoice and go open-minded to interviews with sincerity, because your energy will bring you good results. The Bouquet brings great promise to all those who are willing to fill their hearts with much love and joy. Receive the flowers of destiny in your life and enjoy the good times.

Love and Relationship
Single: For single people, this card promises the appearance of a very loving person who will be source of joy, dreams and promises to become a couple. Enjoy this moment and try to get to know the loved ones closest to you, because maybe it is the love you have been waiting for.

In a Relationship: In love, The Bouquet symbolizes a moment of happiness and accomplishment for a couple. You will enjoy the most complete love and companionship; everything between you will fit perfectly and great achievements can happen, such as the planning of a wedding for those who are waiting for a proposal.

General Aspects
Glory, universal love, altruism, well-being, opportunity, fraternity, optimism, joviality, wisdom and spiritual evolution. Happiness, blessing, contentment, gratitude, love, achievement, maturity, moments of extreme fulfilment, joy and triumph. Healing, understanding, satisfaction, rewards, sincerity, true feelings and loyal friendships. Spiritual ecstasy, protection and times of harmony with favourable results and surprises that arise in many aspects of our life.

Message
Good luck, harvest, surprising gains and fair and sincere exchanges.

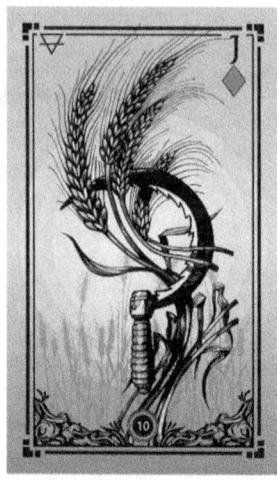

Card 10 - The Sickle

Element ~ Earth

Card 10 of the Gypsy Deck is The Sickle. Although symbolically it represents death, it is a neutral card because its context symbolizes the end of a cycle and transformation. Therefore, its actual value depends on the general context in a complete reading to determine if it is something positive or negative. Here we will address the standard concepts of this feminine energy card.

The shape of the sickle reminds us of the Moon, and in this way we can attribute it to the tender vibrations of women and their capacity for renewal and change. Remember that our journey is really about learning what we need to know to move forward and to go through certain situations in order to become wiser and more complete. That is why transformations are beneficial and necessary. We have a much greater purpose for being fulfilled in this world and so the sickle in the Gypsy Deck pushes us to modify our trajectory and to find what is important for us to gather in this Universe. It is also important to note that after a cut we have the harvest, so it is at that (future) time you will experience the happiness that you were really looking for.

Major Arcana
With its sharp blade the sickle cuts off abruptly where it passes, interrupting developments, whether they are good or bad. It gives you the possibility of rebirth, a new beginning, so you can put yourself on a path that will lead you to victories and success, or sadly it could also signal the end of something that you would like to last in your life.

Minor Arcana

The image on the Jack of Diamonds card is of a young man with a fearless expression, showing solidity and courage. Opportunities will soon be in front of you; all you have to do is to reason wisely to discover the direction. Do not bite off more than you can chew, be sensible and enjoy the achievements.

Interaction between the Arcana

The Sickle announces disruptions, discord, financial loss, job loss, or sometimes the end of a relationship. It can signal death when followed by the coffin card, a life stage that is ending, it may be a good or a bad phase. It most definitely indicates a change of circumstances. The Jack of Diamonds shows the presence of a young man, full of energy, but immature and with a sickle-like nature - harsh, brutal and brutally honest. This card indicates cycles of life through which we pass in an eternal coming and going. It also warns us to be cautious in every way, including love, at work, in business and so on.

Positive Aspects

Changes will come, cycles will be interrupted, and you will be forced to follow new directions. The good news is that this new path will lead you to great moments, full of joy, success and contemplation. The transformation is more than necessary and will lead you toward achieving your goals. Don't be afraid of the new and invest once again in the possibilities that will arise and mark your path with good energy. The positive side of this card is where the other cards in the spread can lead you to. If it is a neutral card, its value will only be discovered when added to the attributes of the other cards. This is a great time to enjoy what you have been given and live in peace of mind and spirit. Allow yourself to renew.

Negative Aspects

A sudden cut is likely to happen in your life which will possibly bring you sorrow. A sudden occurrence will totally change the horizon, leaving you disoriented and without motivation. This card is presented negatively when you have a spread that includes other cards that show obstacles. Its symbolism is a sudden change; whether it will be positive or negative depends on the surrounding cards.

Work and Finances

Changes and transformations may occur in the work environment, or at the site itself. If there isn't much love around, be alert as anything can make your situation difficult in the workplace at this time. It can also indicate the arrival of a new position, a salary increase, good business (if you have your own investment) and even a change of job. If you're unemployed, be prepared, as this card promises to bring you great chances of getting the job you dreamed of. Be aware that good energies will guide you! The Sickle indicates a time to renew and accept the new, for it is necessary. Whether it will bring happiness or momentary bitterness do not lose the focus of your life, which is to achieve true happiness. The Universe will lead you.

Love and Relationship
Single: The Sickle represents an unexpected arrival. Were you in a deep disillusionment? It may be your time to believe again, for a possible love will arise.
In a Relationship: Indicates a change in the relationship, the interpretation you can consider by analysing the moment you currently live in. If you are hoping for one more step in your union for example, it may be that this goal comes to fruition. With a positive card close by in the spread, it can indicate a change because of the arrival of a child, a trip that will change the mood between the couple, a more harmonious and solid delivery or some event that will positively transform your lives. If there is a negative symbolism, The Sickle may indicate the need for separation, which will come to fruition. Perhaps you really need this push to follow your path on the roads that are most beneficial to you. Do not look at the end as something overwhelming, as this situation may present you more interesting possibilities in your life.

General Aspects
Transformation, opening doors and a new era of freedom from current suffering. Detach from your fears, internal and practical transformations. The anxiety will have an end. A period of re-valuation, reformulation and a growth process. Temporary worries and positive renovation. Cut off evil energies, negative people, complainers and gossipers.

Message
Timeout is welcome in our lives and transformations are necessary. If we don't sacrifice things voluntarily, the universe will impose the re-evaluation for us.

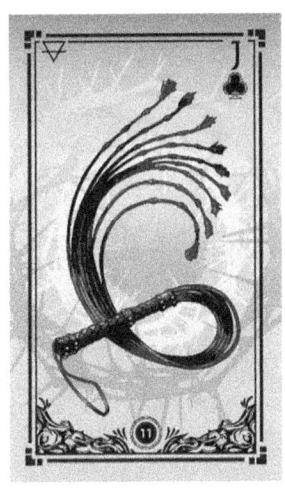

Card 11 - The Whip

Element ~ Earth

The Whip is a symbol of strength and is card 11 of the Gypsy Deck. Its representation is neutral. Your interpretation for this card will be determined by the cards that accompany it in your spread. The Whip is a tool that enhances the strength of the card it accompanies. It is linked to justice and the power to decide, thus representing a higher position. This card gives the person its full power in action to reap the rewards. The Whip is a weapon that will act according to your will and actions. At this point you will have the power to decide outstanding and important issues. Enjoy the energy of this card and try to organize what interests you. Be brave and you will achieve your goals. The strength of The Whip can be used as an aid of the spiritual plan in your life. Now is a great time to take advantage of this energy and increase your self-knowledge.

At this time, you will find resolutions to your problems when you look within to find the answers. Commit yourself to your life with strength and willpower to reap great results. The Master number 11 that comes with this card indicates that you still have much to learn.

Major Arcana
There are very few people who look at The Whip and thinks it's a good thing. And it really is not, it can refer to pain, which can be physical or psychological. The Whip card shows an image of torture, which can come from anywhere, including your inner self.

Minor Arcana

The Jack of Clubs represents a smart and clever young man linked to mystical and spiritual knowledge. When this suit was created in the Middle Ages, this card represented Lancelot, the faithful squire of King Arthur. In the traditional card he carries a shield and a spear which are symbols of a warrior. He appears by The Whip to advise you that you are responsible for the victories or defeats in your life, and he reminds you that everything can be changed.

Interaction between the Arcana

Often when something goes wrong, rather than accept the blame we try to shift it onto other people. The Jack of Clubs intertwined with the Whip reminds us that we have the strength to take control of our lives and solve our own problems. It takes courage and determination not to keep looking back. It is time to stop complaining and being a victim or a martyr. This card can also represent a person who represses himself and does not express himself as much as he would like. It is time to take steps out of this cycle and if necessary seek help from a specialist.

Positive Aspects

The Whip card works as a weapon in your hands to do what is right. If you do use it for good deeds, your path will be well directed, and you'll find the desired balance at the end of the course. It assures you of power and autonomy; do not delay, act now and take control of the situation. Remember though, although you have an important decision to be made quickly, it is important that you don't fail to reflect first, for no one should be misjudged or prejudiced along the way. Your mental power will be very strong at this time and it will point you in the best direction. Connect to your spiritual world to find answers.

Negative Aspects

This card, when presented on its negative side, represents the pursuit of what you want without considering consequences. Ambition will speak louder than reason at this time and you may be tempted to act without any great effort, contemplation or regard what effect it can have on other people. Misuse of power is attributed to this. It is possible to commit injustice and not feel guilty for these actions. In this period, people with spiritual weakness sometimes seek black magic to achieve their goals without any remorse. Be very careful and do not forget the Law of Return.

Work and Finances
The Whip asks for justice. Don't be stern with co-workers and always think calmly. This card warns you of possible fights in this environment, so do not engage in conversations that are not your business. If you can't avoid confrontation, draw on your spiritual power to lessen tension and calm the situation. If you're unemployed, your outlook will be the key to success, consciously make the effort to think positively. The Whip brings the message that you are responsible for planting today what you will reap tomorrow, it will give you the strength to act, but use this wisdom only for good things because the moment of judgment always comes to everyone. Beware of unnecessary expenses in times of financial stress. Do not be a victim, take your situation and act with responsibility.

Love and Relationship
Single: You are likely to be wanting a relationship currently but have been too guarded. You must recognize this problem and strive for it to be solved, calmly and sensitively. You may need the help of a therapist to overcome the pains of the past and allow yourself to live in the present.

In a Relationship: Care must be taken not to boycott the relationship. Consider the situation calmly, for a new person may appear in your life. Either you or your partner are likely to be accepting the current situation out of fear of the result of taking action. This is likely to drag on if no one takes steps to resolve the issue. The solution should be one that will bring the happiness to both parties. Reflect on the issue and communicate with each other; if necessary, seek help from a counsellor.

General Aspects
Strength, the need for balance between reason and instincts, mind, controlling forces, mental magic that can build or destroy, efforts committed to achieve goals and objectives. Self-punishment, aggressiveness, arguments, possessiveness and sadomasochism. Thought, intelligence, and agility must be utilised to develop positive qualities within ourselves. Human instincts, flesh, ardent desire, sexuality and vitality. Dogmas, restlessness, authority, authoritarianism, exaggeration, disputes, abuse of power and imposition.

Message
Energies that must be committed to progress, control, mastery, ability to overcome challenges. The strength and inner power to resist the obstacles and continue the journey.

Card 12 - The Birds

Element ~ Air

The Birds, or the Bird is card number 12 of the Gypsy Deck and it appears in a reading to remind you of the good that is freedom. Birds sing their beautiful songs when they are free to go in the direction they wish. The Birds card can come as advice to be like a free bird, to follow your life with great faith and without limiting yourself to only seeing beautiful horizons. It also says that we must learn to live with others to find true harmony and reminds us that we are more likely to be happy in the company of others rather than alone, as we can exchange experiences and feelings to define the directions of life.

A further message from this card tells us that we should not allow ourselves to live in a "prison", or in the shadow of others. When we're supressed or oppressed, giving up our dreams and freedom, we will reach a point where we no longer know how to make our own life decisions, just as the bird that lives caged for a long time will no longer know how to survive in the real world if it is set free. Never forget your life goals. And remember that freedom is one of your greatest assets. Learn to share and walk alongside valiant people who are important, do not hold back or limit yourself. Fear only diminishes us to something we are not.

When it comes to health, it asks you to be aware of problems of stress and depression. Do not sink, react!

Major Arcana
There are many species of birds, and each has special characteristics. Owls for example represent wisdom, prudence and observation. Swallows are never alone, they are always with their flock. If we think about it in general, birds represent hope and freedom. When free, their singing is beautiful and we love to listen to it, but if they get trapped or lonely their song is sad because they long for freedom.

Minor Arcana
The Seven of Diamonds represents the moment of reflection on what has happened so far. Often results takes time to arrive, but it is no use to exhaust your energies in the expectation of harvesting what you have planted before the right season arrives. It takes patience and reassurance, because everything happens in time.

Interaction between the Arcana
It is necessary to work on any anxiety, don't be impulsive, be conscious of the balance between working together with others and freedom. For those who are very dependent, it is necessary to dare to be more independent. If you usually want to do everything yourself, now is the time for you to learn to work with others in order to grow. Be careful not to use all of your energy impulsively. The Birds neutralize The Snake card.

Positive Aspects
The Birds card is a warning about the way we lead our lives. It stresses the importance of giving value to our power of choice, but at the same time not forgetting that we also depend on others to evolve and achieve what we want. Working well in partnership or a group in this period will yield great fruit as we are always learning in life and others can teach us a great deal. It also reminds us that we should not lower ourselves to the point where we are no longer ourselves; this journey will only have a meaningful connection to others if we allow ourselves to run after our own dreams.

Negative Aspects
The negative side of the card warns of exaggerations. Do not limit yourself too much, nor be too individualistic. Lack of balance is keeping you at a distance from achieving what you crave. Control and learn to enjoy all the good energies the Universe and people transmit to you.

Work and Finances

For those who work or have their own business, this is the time to head in and dare, but always seek help from like-minded people with similar interests and prioritize teamwork, as these will benefit you greatly. If you're unemployed, you need to understand that the information you acquired in your last job is nothing but information for your life. It is time to let go of old ideals so that you can position yourself properly in the market. The Birds card depicts a person who does not tend to venture into the business world alone or who prefers to work with others. You need to pay attention to finances and have backup plans for your source of income.

Love and Relationship

Single: This card is a reminder that having fun is a part of life too. You are right in not wanting to enter a relationship with anyone at this time, allow yourself to enjoy life more and get distracted until the right person appears.

In a Relationship: Anyone in a relationship should be very cautious at this time. Now is not the time to be arguing. Being submissive or demanding too much just wears out the happiness in a relationship. Always seek harmony; this attitude will do you good only.

General Aspects

Happiness, joy, contentment, romance, victory, freedom, enthusiasm, triumph, realized desires, surprises, love, tenderness, luck, truth and harmony. Need to pay more attention to the simple things of life, to feelings, spirituality, purity, good intentions, warmth, joviality, companionship and the help that comes without waiting. The positive news and energies visit us as a breath of fresh air. Protection, courage, elegance, softness and beauty. The soul flies in pursuit of its dreams deeper and realizes them with will and determination. The song chants the accomplishments, but without announcing passing events. Freedom, new horizons, daring, simplicity, travel and happy adventures. It shows that we can go far beyond the common or known horizons.

Message

Birds indicate spirituality and the higher states of soul consciousness.

Card 13 - The Child

Element ~ Water

Card 13 of the Gypsy Deck is a positive card. The Child represents innocence and hope in the childish gaze. In a reading, this card indicates that someone young will make you think about your life and see that plans and visions you have about the future are far more interesting than how you currently see them. We are often attached to thoughts shaped by our experiences which cause us to restrict ourselves and we end up limiting ourselves to dreaming and really reaching some goal.

The Child is sincerely happy, non-judgemental, and enjoys every moment as if he or she possessed some magic. Children are always looking for possibilities and are generally not afraid to venture into the unknown or to question what is happening. When bad events appear in life, a child usually learns how to get around or over them and their smile is never usually far away, even amid the difficulties. This card reminds you how important it is not to impose limits, that you need not judge anyone, nor be judged by another to grow. You simply need to believe you are capable and strive to be so. This is the shortest and most sincere way to achieve success.

Major Arcana
This card speaks of new beginnings, innocence, optimism and the joy of living. It can also reflect irresponsibility, absence of fears and prejudices, fragility and immaturity. The child is spontaneous, quiet, focused, and unintentional. Children don't normally conceal thoughts, they are always open to the world

and able to experience each new event without barriers or prejudices. They are fascinated and willing to learn everything that is taught. We cannot forget that this energy has free transit in the spiritual world: "If you do not change and become like children, you will by no means enter the kingdom of God." Only the original condition - undefined, fresh and vital, but vulnerable and insecure - symbolized by a child, is open to development.

Minor Arcana

The Jack of Spades indicates that you must be vigilant and attentive to what is going on around you. Often the Jacks, whichever suit they are, indicate a young person who is close to us. One who will likely influence a certain part of our life. This card may also concern the person asking the question, indicating that he or she should maintain an active stance in the face of events.

Interaction between the Arcana

The Child card can also symbolize the children of the person consulting or a child yet to be born. The Jack of Spades warns that the spontaneity of the child is not always welcome in more serious matters. Speaking without thinking can be a disaster, which generates fights, gossip and misunderstandings. There is a thin line between spontaneous and impulsive.

Positive Aspects

The message of the card is a reminder to allow your inner child to guide you at this time. Don't allow fear or anxieties to hold back or defer goals. And remember, if what you are attempting doesn't work, you still have learned something new. If it does work, congratulations! If we could overcome problems with the outlook of a child, we would spend our lives constantly evolving and smiling, we would be able to respond in the best way to the worst moments. If you are looking for something new in your life, be it professionally or love, this card indicates that it is time to take a risk and invest in the ideas you have in mind. Your creativity and open mind on current issues will help you find the best paths and answers. Broaden your vision and knowledge, free yourself from the common fears and prejudices in the environment in which we live. Curiosity can show you more interesting answers than you had imagined.

Negative Aspects

The Child asks you to be careful not to let the excess spoil this moment. Do not be immature and remember your responsibilities, never neglect them.

Work and Finances

Beware of the naivety in the work environment, some people may abuse your apparent innocence. On the other hand, enjoy this moment to learn even more from experiences. If you are currently unemployed, focus on your dreams and life projects, but take a more serious stand during interviews. The Child is a beautiful card that brings a lot of positive energy, harmony and happiness to your life. Enjoy this moment.

Love and Relationship

Single: Your energy will enchant the people around you. It is quite possible that a new love will come into your life attracted by this charismatic air. Beware of false friendships that can hurt your emotions, avoid subjects that may turn out to be gossipy.

In a Relationship: The message greatly depends on which other cards appear with it, but it may be a sign of a pregnancy. If any problems arise in the relationship at this time, they will be small and easily overcome, have no fears.

General Aspects

Sincerity, beauty, renovation, harmony, childhood, ludic, love, friendship, new things, spontaneity, transparency, naivety, truth and energy. Lack of fears or over fears. Good feelings, children, a new child or a pregnancy. Surprises, happiness and new cycles will be lived without suffering. In the other side, this card advises us to be aware of lack of responsibility or immaturity in the face of serious situations. It is necessary to be open for new teachings and have a true willingness to experience new situations.

Message

We should allow the enthusiasm and optimism of our inner child to conduct us constantly on our life journey. This is an invitation to be open for the world's experiences.

Card 14 - The Fox

Element ~ Air

On its own, The Fox card in the Gypsy Deck wants to teach us agility, cleverness and wit. It can be an omen of a negative experience in your life or simply a boring situation you need to deal with.

The Fox indicates that an unexpected situation is likely to arise, even if everything seems to be going very well. This scenario that will form will not always be your fault, it may also be a trap of the life that was in your path. The image on this card is of an animal that does not appear to have a friendly countenance. The animal seems to be on the prowl, waiting for the right moment to attack. With great cunning and agility, The Fox usually appears at a decisive moment in which the prey is vulnerable.

Major Arcana
The Fox uses a strategy to hunt and leaves no trace, so this card alerts us to people of dubious character, betrayals, pitfalls, pranks, liars and cheats who take advantage of everything. This card asks you to be careful and cautious. A fox waiting for his hunt is what brings this arcane. The Fox presents a situation of difficult resolution, one you will likely have trouble dealing with. It can be demonstrative of a trap or ambush. In most cases, this card is more targeted at situations than people. The Fox is a predator and therefore represents the capacity for observation and cunning.

Minor Arcana

In analysing the Nine of Clubs card, we can see that it suggests mental balance and control of the energies that favour creation of the necessary conditions to overcome problems and make decisions. It is a synonym for insight, good judgment and ideal perception of what surrounds you, without losing restraint and keeping a defensive position if necessary. This wisdom reveals inspiration at its best and empowers positive use of energies, enhances philanthropic qualities and helps make dreams a reality.

Interaction between the Arcana

The Fox card speaks of wit, cleverness, speed and flexibility of our actions, often fundamental to our survival and advises us to be cautious. This is a time to be wary of becoming a victim of unscrupulous and opportunistic people who may cause us serious moral or financial loss. False proposition and cunning gallantry may result in involvement in difficult situations for us. Symbolically, The Fox embodies the contradictions inherent in human nature - active and inventive, but at the same time destructive; independent, audacious and controversially fearful. It is also attributed to great longevity.

Positive Aspects

Quite often, The Fox appears as a warning to act cautiously, no matter how dangerous your way seems. There are likely to be pitfalls, and you will suffer serious damage if you do not watch out. Use the wisdom and cleverness of The Fox to circumvent situations. Depending on how the card is surrounded in the spread, it generally represents the attributes of The Fox in the query. That is, you have a cunning spirit, who knows how to seize the opportunities and is very smart for the events that surround him, just waiting for the right moment to "get in the picture."

Negative Aspects

You may become victim of a betrayal. Usually the problem that this card presents is related to events in life, but it can alert us of possible betrayal by someone close to you. The Fox bringing this message tells this betrayal will be something planned, premeditated. Do not be naive and evaluate everyone around you, do not over-commit yourself to people you do not know, and be sure of the loyalty of those who have been in your life for a long time.

Work and Finances
Be careful with co-workers at this time as a situation in which you can be a victim may arise. Try not to talk too much about other people or situations. Wait for this period to pass and avoid friction and gossip. You may have been envied by someone you considered a friend and in fact was all this time plotting to bring you down. An unexpected event is likely to happen, and it is a good time for you to be The Fox, take notice of little signs that should come your way, do not allow yourself to be inattentive. Be careful about the things you say and with whom you speak to. Reassess your friends, stay focused on your love relationship and let life follow your flow. Remember to keep your eye on details that can tear you down emotionally and/or financially.

Love and Relationship
Single: Meeting someone is not a problem at this time but finding someone ideal is not quite so easy. This is a time for the right strategy and games to be able to build a successful relationship.

In a Relationship: Evaluate the situation in which you live, perhaps you are in a carousel of lies. If you are asking about a current relationship, this card may appear as a warning that your partner may be disloyal. This is not a time to get into a crisis of jealousy or paranoia, just watch carefully and distrust if necessary. It will soon be apparent if the relationship is healthy and it is worthwhile maintaining the necessary bonds of trust.

General Aspects
It is a scourge, traps, deceit, lies, cunning, prejudice, eventuality, illusory gallantry that leads to losses, plans, robbery, someone who tries to be what they are not. This is a time to insist on something or someone to benefit and above all take advantage. This card warns of the worries and dangers we may face in certain situations or even of the people around us. The enemies or moments of loss through traps in which we fall for trusting dishonest and disloyal people. There is the warning and the need to plan our goals well. It reminds us to be careful with illicit business, malice, cold hearts, calculated attitudes. However, it reveals that there is still enough of the inexhaustible energy for all goals and objectives to be maintained, so internal resources must be used to continue the advancement of its path.

Message
Much falsehood is in the air, the individual should work to improve the gift of strategy.

Card 15 - The Bear

Element ~ Earth

Card 15 of the Gypsy Deck, The Bear, comes to alert you to pay close attention to the people with whom you live or who surround you. The Bear represents betrayal and warns that someone may try to take advantage of some weakness of yours. Do not overload yourself, you may be worried about events that have happened recently but know that acting out of desperation is as inefficient as doing nothing. Face any obstacle that comes up head on, stand tall and do not be afraid, you will overcome any difficulty this way. If you let problems accumulate, even small ones, they will cause you more trouble in the future and you will feel as though you are carrying the world on your back. So, in order not to wear out, focus on a certain pending subject and eliminate them one by one from your life.

The Bear as an animal is a large, strong creature which does not detract from its agility at all; so, a great deal of focus is needed when approaching it. This symbolism is reflected in the card, be careful not to share too much of your personal information with people and be careful not to leave pending matters that anyone can use to harm you. In health this card asks you to be very attentive with excesses which can destabilize your physical and mental health.

Major Arcana
Rest assured that when the Gypsy Deck was created, there were no teddy bears. As much as card artists can make it look like a friendly bear, remember that in real life they are wild animals, extremely aggressive when their territory is

invaded. Although large and heavy, the bear is quite agile, and can viciously attack its enemy with a simple swipe. However, it is wise to remember that many bears have been tamed, which is the specialty of the gypsy Ursari clan. Solving a big problem or getting into balance in troubled times is like taming a bear.

Minor Arcana

The Ten of Clubs card indicates excesses, could be in responsibilities or even just an arduous task. Care must be taken not to exhaust the energies. You must be aware of the limits, and if necessary ask for help.

Interaction between the Arcana

Face the problems ahead and do not get carried away by the fear of not solving them. Otherwise, you will accumulate situations which can lead you to exhaustion. The Bear card speaks of excesses, so be careful about everything that is too much: work, jealousy, care, or carelessness. Strive to find balance with wisdom and courage.

Positive Aspects

The Bear with all his strength also represents the inner wisdom adviser with the power to defend himself if he has the mindset to take the right actions. It symbolizes protection, which may come through a spiritual form, or a friend that sincerely loves you. When friends notice you are going through a troubled period they will be more inclined to help you with a more active brotherly or sisterly spirit.

Negative Aspects

Someone is waiting for the right moment to attack. The problem is that it is not clear where the betrayal will come from. It may be from someone you least expect, or from someone you do not have much contact with but who envies you for something. Keep watch and be especially careful not to overload yourself because that will lower your awareness and be your main weakness right now.

Work and Finances

Do not submit to excess, you are important, but overload will only weaken you. You will find it harder to deal with situations if even your health is threatened by your lack of control. It's no use getting away from life's problems by burying yourself in work, so be careful. Value yourself in your life! If you are unemployed, this is the time to calm down and re-evaluate your career so far in the professional area. Take some time for yourself, start a course if you prefer, but be sure about what you want when looking for something new.

The Bear card warns you not to give in to excesses in any area of your life, attempts to fix problems in this way will only overload you and will not solve anything efficiently. Take time for yourself, relax, rest, clear the mind and ease the process of reasoning. Be very careful of false friendships.

Love and Relationship

Single: What has stopped you so far from meeting someone is the fear of suffering again. The wounds of a past relationship are haunting you still. Let go of those moments that are gone and prepare your heart to receive new feelings.

In a Relationship: For any type of relationship, this card passes the message that you need to avoid disagreements with your partner. Fighting at this time will greatly disadvantage the couple. If you are married, try to talk more with your partner, you appear to have been distant recently and the relationship needs this communication, contact and reciprocal affection. If you date, or the relationship seems to be compromised in any way, limit your jealousy and the feeling that you are the owner of your partner. This situation is becoming overwhelming for both and no one will ever own anyone.

General Aspects

Coldness, magic, fetish, irrationality, evil eye, explosion, envy, desire, misfortune, hibernation, losses, aggression, malefic energies, falsehood, anguish, agony, agitation, violent and opportunistic passions, negative influences of the astral or of malicious people, plagues, lies, illusions, spite, treachery, jealousy, petty interests, and selfishness. The Bear card warns about the need for spiritual cleansing. Dive into the shadows themselves so that you can rise above the instinctive wild forces.

Message

Falsehood, anguish and the need to take care of personal power. Avoid substances you can abuse. Face your fears instead of trying a quick escape.

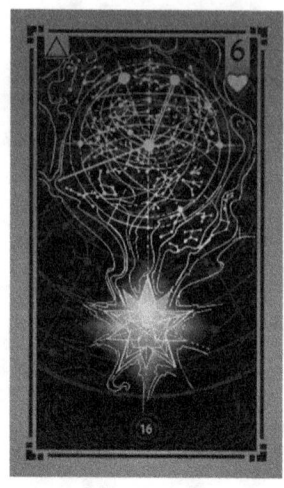

Card 16 - The Star

Element ~ Fire

The Star card in the Gypsy Deck is connected to faith, spirituality and religious pursuits, and bodes well for issues related to the spiritual plane and friends. Being linked to the Cups in tarot it carries deep knowledge related to the emotions, feelings and powers of the heart. The suit of hearts is associated with the element of water, which governs our options, unconditional love, purification, blessings and balance.

The Star card carries the number sixteen, the numerological sum of which is seven. This is the number of the perfection and totality of the Universe, and it is also associated with the mysteries of occultism, spirituality, and mysticism. The Star represents the harmony between the four elements of nature: earth, air, fire and water; as well as the Spirit and the fifth element. Many religious groups use the five-pointed star, or pentagram, as an expression of union. Although you may not know it yet, it is likely that you have the gift of healing. It is advisable to perform meditation because you are not yet ready to perform voluntary work, but soon you will find your way.

Major Arcana

The Star represents our brilliance. It appears to reaffirm the confidence in oneself, to hope for the future and always to look forward to the best, it is the path blessed by the Heavenly Father. The energy of The Star brings us inner peace and balance. Listening to what the heart has to tell us is one of the lessons to be learned from this card.

Minor Arcana

The Six of Hearts carries lunar energy, which symbolizes the dream of love, idealization in various aspects. You need to be careful not to fall into delusions. On the other hand, it also represents the inner child, without fears; or even the will to live. In a positive sense, this card shows that innocence can often bring optimism to overcoming obstacles.

Interaction between the Arcana

If you want to be a star it is important to have a foundation, but it cannot be just your creativity on its own. As difficult as the present situation may be, everything is just lessons to be learned in order to strengthen faith in self and in higher powers.

Positive Aspects

The Star card suggests that it is time to free yourself from the past, to have confidence in yourself and to use your spirituality to find the best paths in your life. Difficult times can still come but it is important to know that it is through this transition that you will certainly achieve your own brilliance as The Star. Best of all, embrace that you are capable, your self-esteem is high and through creativity, inspiration and a bit of luck (which is present in this period of your life) you will get the results you dream of.

Negative Aspects

Do not try to live in the past; you do not need this sustenance to grow in life. Let go of what no longer adds to your path, do not let dreams take you too far from reality, and most importantly, do not let anything diminish your value and brilliance.

Work and Finances

In work and finances, you should be a little careful because your current brightness may annoy the people who work with you. They may make you feel insecure because of their own envy, and just as a star does, you should strengthen yourself in your light. At the same time, the card indicates that your managers may see your brightness as positive for business. Your star will brighten the work environment, and those who can understand your qualities will positively boost you to develop more each day. If you are unemployed, this is your time to shine and stand out among the other candidates. Trust and bet on your potential. The Star card brings very deep symbolism about the impression people have of you. It is essential that you allow yourself to develop and make everyone see your potential.

Love and Relationship
Single: The Star card shows that this may be a good time for a new relationship. It is important not to have any unresolved situations with other people in the past. It is fundamental that the old is left behind so that the new can be established.

In a Relationship: If you are dating, it is possible that your partner feels a little insecure about their brightness, independence and pace of life. If married, remember that it is important not to allow the relationship to be too conservative or adventurous, getting out of routine will bring more joy and lightness. If you want to better understand something related to your partner, encourage him/her to talk about their feelings and to share those feelings more with you. Your perceptions are also important currently.

General Aspects
Illumination, luck, spiritual strength, grants, protection, new life, evolution, perfection, optimism, hope, faith, protection, good influences, powerful energies and exaltation. Motivation, confidence and progress - difficulties that are overcome. Happiness, harmony, peace, balance, courage, spiritual treasure, love and affection. It also guides us to take care of our personal brilliance and self-image. What is predestined in our lives, the awakening, and the spiritual link that positively unites us with some situations or people. Spiritual growth. This card in some cases may indicate the excess of starriness and glamour.

Message
Enlighten, luck, new possibilities and spiritual fulfilment.

Card 17 - The Stork

Element ~ Air

The Stork is card 17 of the Gypsy Deck, which brings a great energy of will to make love work and overcome any barrier. It indicates that you are a sweet, sensitive and very generous person, and will use all these attributes to build lasting and peaceful relationships. However, when we talk about relationships and love it is not only about what involves two people, it can be any activity that has a lot of importance in your life and will do you good.

The Stork promises success and achievement of something very good to be experienced that will happen unexpectedly. It may be a new love, or the fulfilment of a relationship that you longed for, peace in your current relationship, prosperity in investments and work and even a trip that will fill you with good memories and joy. When it comes to health, this card indicates recovery from illness. Good weather is right there in front of you, positive changes will come, so do not miss the opportunity to be happy.

Major Arcana
A symbol of fertility, The Stork represents the arrival of good news. As they build their nests in high places, the European peasants had the custom of preparing platforms on their roofs so that storks would settle there and bring fertility and prosperity to the house. The Stork is a monogamist animal, and it means family. When this card appears in a spread, it can suggest a person concerned with material issues. However, this is due to their concerns for well-being, not just for money.

Minor Arcana

The Queen of Hearts is a sweet and loving woman who is intuitive, generous, careful, wise and romantic, but unpredictable. This card can represent the power of fulfilment through love.

Interaction between the Arcana

It is a card that balances the earth and water elements. Desires of prosperity and love. It is the fulfilment of good things: altruism, generosity and love. The good things that are coming. The gift that the future holds for you will be unexpected and very welcome. It could be a journey, relocation to a new home, innovation at work or even pregnancy.

Positive Aspects

This card is very positive and indicates the emergence of good times in your life. The Stork symbolizes surrender to something unexpected, which will totally change your path for the better. Following its pure concept in tales, The Stork can also symbolize the arrival of a baby. If your dream was to have a child, be it from your own gestation or adoption process, this card says that the energies are favourable for this to come to fruition. So, live open-mindedly waiting for results because when we least expect, the Universe conspires in our favour and gives us wonderful gifts that we often did not even think we deserved.

Negative Aspects

Regarding health, when The Stork comes accompanied by a negative card it can symbolize problems with breasts, hormones and thyroid.

Work and Finances

The Stork symbolizes something positive and unexpected popping up in the business world. Possibly some money you will receive, whether you are employed or unemployed. It may be a new opportunity, a new proposal, a new job, a promotion, or a special project that will earn you a bonus. It indicates some very positive form of success. This card carries a very positive energy, filled with prosperity and good news. Gains are about to happen unexpectedly, which will bring you great joy and a sense of achievement.

Love and Relationship

Single: At this stage you are highly likely to find someone who will brighten your days. It's advisable that you do not totally surrender to this passion without care, the hormones are conspiring for an easy pregnancy, stay alert.

In a Relationship: For those in a relationship, the stork promises good times between the couple. Much romanticism and dedication will be present in unforgettable moments. This is a great time to take that trip for two that you wanted so much. But if it is not part of your plans currently, be very careful not to get pregnant.

General Aspects

Novelty, surprise, news, something new happening soon, new paths, news, pregnancy, something unprecedented and surprising. Purity, peace, happiness, harmony, travel, acceptance of life, opportunities, good omens, revelations and adventures. An invitation to glimpse into the future and leave the past behind. New challenges and courage to face life. Liveliness and freedom from pain and suffering.

Message

The life that is announced with new joys. Good omens.

Card 18 - The Dog

Element ~ Water

The Dog card symbolizes loyalty, companionship, understanding and alertness. Originally in the Gypsy cards the image would be that of a horse since having a pet in Romani communities is extremely uncommon. All the characteristics highlighted represent the old Gypsy symbolism for The Horse which was changed to The Dog when the cards were westernized. The fundamental characteristics and meaning that represent this card remain the same. The Dog is a positive card that indicates the presence of true friends, those who appear to support us and help without expecting anything in return for what they do.

Depending on the combinations of the spread, The Dog may symbolize the need for spiritual protection. It suggests that self-knowledge will be very important to develop at this time. In general, this card represents the arrival of something special, such as a celebration of something that will be realized. It also symbolizes long-lasting and secure relationships, as it is represented by the most reliable animal that does everything to please. You will feel much fulfilled by having special people in your life and you will want to dedicate your time to those who are loved by you, friends or family members. This is likely to be a period of good health, but the arcane also reminds you that it is necessary to keep moving, group activities are welcome and will bring you great pleasure.

In the Gypsy Deck the meaning of each card depends on the other cards that accompany it in the spread. The Dog card by itself does not have any negative aspects, even appearing with cards that are negative it gives the message that you will not be alone and can count on faithful friends even in the most complicated moments in life.

Major Arcana
The Dog is a faithful friend, the one you can always count on in your life. It represents the purity of feelings, trust, friendship, companionship and loyalty.

Minor Arcana
The Ten of Hearts represents happiness and fulfilment in love. It shows us that long-lasting relationships can be had and we can achieve our goals. When The Dog appears in a reading, we are likely to feel an even greater satisfaction than usual by spending time with loved ones, be they friends or family. Love is manifested in a harmonious way, and it favours us in relationships in general.

Interaction between the Arcana
Expect a time for celebration of the good moments to appear as the result of an important situation in your life. Love is flowing in all areas of your life. Even if it is not in its best phase, be calm, soon will come the moment of great achievements. Although other cards in the reading may be challenging, the presence of The Dog evidences that there will be positive changes in your life, mostly coming from friends.

Positive Aspects
You are loved, your way of living has earned you very loyal friends on whom you can count for the rest of your life. They are people so dear that they are happy to go to great lengths to see you and expect nothing in return. So, if you are going through some challenging moments, count on the support of someone who shows interest in making sure that you well.

Negative Aspects
The Dog card does not carry any negative energy and in a reading with negative cards it is a reminder that you are not alone, you will be supported by your loved ones. The Dog card also suggests that there will be positive changes which will happen due to the help of special people around you. This card can warn you against co-dependency in an unhealthy relationship and may also be a reminder that you need to be more active, a lonely and bored dog is not a happy dog.

Work and Finances
If you are employed, The Dog card indicates that you are a faithful employee and that you are committed to your duties. You will grow through merit and

dedication. This card brings a great message for your life! Enjoy and open your heart to those who deserve to be valued, because they will not think twice to help you when you need it. If you are unemployed or looking to change jobs, friendships will probably give you a little push. People who really like you will advise you of the best way to get what you want.

Love and Relationship

Single: You quite possibly have someone very close to you, who you see as a friend, although he or she sees you as someone very special and would like to take the friendship further. If not, it won't be long before someone new comes into your life. Be sure to look closely at friends first, it is up to you to interpret how deep this feeling really is.

In a Relationship: This card is very positive, it indicates that you are complete in everything, have a harmonious union and fidelity and companionship are above anything.

General Aspects

Loyalty, friendship, companionship, truth, support of loyal people we can count on. We will have help, respect, purity, feelings, honesty, affection, unconditional love, humility, wisdom, cleverness, agility, defence, meaningful protection that brings luck and joy. Happy and harmonious relationship, sincerity, an ally, someone who defends us from the dangers of life, confidence, serenity and dignity.

Message

The Dog card always suggests signs of good things that will bring progress and joy, whether through someone or some situation. Compassion is guaranteed but avoid co-dependency.

Card 19 – The Tower

Element ~ Fire

Self-knowledge and spiritual elevation. The Tower card means a moment of reflection for you. It is time to restructure and learn to separate what strengthens you and what can bring you down.

The Tower asks for a moment of meditation and analysis of life. A great deal will be discovered to help you follow the best direction and set the best goals. This will also help clarify who adds value and who diminishes you in this journey. You will be more structured and empowered to take the necessary actions, thus realizing your projects. This card is great news for everyone, because introspection will bring you the necessity to understand the challenges of life and determine the focus for this moment and your plans.

Major Arcana
Unlike the meaning of The Tower in regular tarot decks, this card refers to our true selves, our connection to the spiritual world. From the top of a tower we are closer to the sky and can see everything, from approaching danger to birds flying high along their path.

Minor Arcana
The Ten of Spades is one of the arcana that is not very positive, although it is not all negative. It is necessary to know how to interpret as this card can mean depression, travel or certain loss of energy. It can suggest a loss of some kind and at times suggests grief and sadness can appear.

Interaction between the Arcana

First, The Tower is related to spirituality and our inner world, indicating that perhaps it is time to retreat to discover something about us. It can be our mission, or just one aspect that we should improve on our journey. It may still be related to our Karma. It is the moment of introspection and search that no one can do for us or help us with. Collected within ourselves, we reveal who we truly are, stripped of the masks of the social and material world.

Positive Aspects

The positive side of The Tower card in the Gypsy Deck is that it suggests you will be more focused on your own life, with the energy to analyse everything and figure out which way to go. This momentary isolation is the perfect ingredient for you to raise your self-knowledge and bring only beneficial effects to your day to day life. This introspection and focus will ensure your senses are more accurate, and you will be ready to analyse everything around you. Your focus should be yourself at this time, and the quest for the essence of your inner peace. Remember that the more you fortify yourself and stay in balance with life, the more good things will come your way.

Negative Aspects

When presented on a negative side, this card can mean that your isolation is not for your highest good. You are possibly going through a very difficult time after experiencing a big loss which has caused you to cut yourself off from the world; you may have even fallen into depression. Beware of the dark and destructive thoughts that your own mind can create; our head can be our worst enemy if we let it.

Work and Finances

You have a tremendous desire for professional achievement, to achieve a dream or goal and this card will help you to seek the best way. Perhaps personal matters are hindering your professional performance and this card will help you resolve them. The Tower brings you the message that you need to reflect more on yourself to find the answers. Sometimes we have everything right before our eyes but we cannot see because we are looking in the wrong direction. Take advantage of this moment of isolation and introspection. If necessary, redefine the way you live, it is never late to start over, life is yours and you are the one who makes the rules.

Love and Relationship
Single: Destiny will act in your life and if you are alone you will find a person who in a short time will represent a strong bond in your life. You will likely become inseparable quickly and it will feel as though you were always destined to meet.

In a Relationship: If you're in a relationship, this card represents greater affinity and a deeper involvement of love.

General Aspects
Protection, the spiritual world, faith, revaluation, intelligence, essence, astral power, the soul, the self, the truth, detachment from the things of the human and material world, renewal of concepts and values before life, active thinking, studies, research, wisdom, change of opinion, detachment from the past, patience, waiting and abandonment of things that no longer have importance. Balance and structure will happen with healthy isolation. This card is a valuable, important message about everything we can do internally and how much we gain in getting to know ourselves better. It is the representation of the essence of the soul. Humility and respect, the need to listen to the inner voice. Solitude in the form of self-discovery to gain maturity.

Message
Voluntary isolation is important to clarify the way.

Card 20 – The Garden

Element ~ Earth

Card 20 in the Gypsy Deck is The Garden which represents one of our first domains of knowledge. This is because in the religious context, our first contact territory was the Garden of Eden.

This card is represented by the image of a quiet place, often flowery, an environment of perfect harmony and peace. At the same time the garden gives us the feeling of deep knowledge, as if we were accustomed to this landscape, something brought from our childhood, with a welcoming air. We must take care to ensure the garden remains beautiful and flowery. It is necessary that we take care of it, always planting new flowers, watering them so they will grow and expand the territory for even more flowers to appear.

Major Arcana
The Garden is a beautiful place, a warm and relaxing environment. In this place there is peace and it seems that everything we need is there within our reach. Still, we feel incomplete. It is because in The Garden we can reflect on our lives and recognize our limits, but not everything that is presented is concrete or definitive.

Minor Arcana
With the Eight of Spades, we work on our most intimate fears of freeing ourselves from the bonds we put ourselves in, so that we can move forward in

the search for the fulfilment of our desires. This card can also represent conflict, distress or mental confusion.

Interaction between the Arcana

Despite conflicts, confusion or anguish, externally people often appear to be the opposite; we seem to live in a calm and tranquil garden. Something has led people to block their life and their pleasures. It is your right to enjoy what you have earned, and you should not suffer because of it. The Garden card guides you to stop pretending that there are no problems.

Positive Aspects

This card symbolises the return in life of everything that you have planted. It is time to enjoy what you dreamt of all this time and reap the benefits of the 'land' you prepared to receive this happiness. Enjoy the good times, let special people join you and continue to take care of your garden. It is worth remembering that for every action there is a reaction. For every action in pursuit of a goal, rewards will come ind time. We spend long hours, or even years trying to reach goals that may seem unattainable, but believe in your future, the world spins and the hours run so that everything can flourish.

Negative Aspects

If you have not cared for your soul, if you have only planted bad 'seeds' or simply stagnated in life expecting external forces to act for you, The Garden card indicates that you are unlikely to go through a much desired experience at this time. First, you must grow so that you can be on your way to achieving your dreams. If you are in a moment of disappointment, know that this is your opportunity to review your life concepts and change the way you have led your life. Start changing things today so that you will be able to enjoy your beautiful garden tomorrow.

Work and Finances

It's time to be rewarded for all your efforts. The Garden card suggests this is a period of peace and understanding among teammates. Remember to keep being devoted and continue showing strong involvement in your role. If you are unemployed, focus on your goals and strive to achieve what you want, your efforts will be recognized. In the Gypsy Deck, the garden represents gratification for your efforts in life. Never forget to take care of your soul, when it is flowering it will only bring positive energies and much harmony to your life.

Love and Relationship

Single: If you are looking for a connection, you should look at pleasures in life before trying to find the great love. You are likely to have short relationships without much learning at this time. If you are single, don't rush, continue to take care of your 'garden'. As soon as the flowers unleash, all the positive energies will bring a beautiful person into your life.

In a Relationship: This will depend on how well you have been taking care of love in your life. If you already have a partner and have tended this relationship with love and care, this will be a beautiful moment together. Everything you have dedicated to this relationship seems to have yielded good results.

General Aspects

The need to ask the heart about everything that is meaningful and to re-evaluate our life concepts. Wisdom, humility, consolidation of good things, the harvest of everything that had been planted and the seeds that we have sprouted. It is not a positive or negative message card, it is usually neutral. It reminds us how we are capable of planting both goodness and badness in life. It can also announce longevity, efforts and the result of everything we believe in. The Garden brings a message to be attentive to the purest and most beautiful side of life.

Message

Choose the right plant for the right climate with fertile soil and care. It will grow!

Card 21 – The Mountain

Element ~ Earth

The Mountain, card 21 of the Gypsy Deck, carries the message that it is the time when you need to have firmness and conviction in your beliefs to overcome challenges. It may seem to be a frightening challenge card; a mountain can appear as something impossible to overcome. With our dreams on the other side of this challenge, we can have the impression that they will indeed be unreachable. This thought may be heavier than the mountain, learn to see it from a different view. Realize that it is at the top of the mountain where we are closer to the Divine. Its peak is the meeting point between Heaven and Earth.

Have the top of the mountain as the goal; from there you will clearly see the entire horizon, the challenges and the ways out. Focus on the result, not on what you may face along the way, the reward will be much better. Do not forget to strengthen your spiritual side; it will be your base to get to the best point of your life.

Major Arcana
The person who wants to conquer the mountain usually does not think about the challenges that may appear along the way, but only of the result. There is no doubt that the challenge is immense, and therefore we must be aware of our limits. You must be flexible to achieve your goals. You need to be careful and perseverant, so that the summit can be reached. And when you do reach it, the reward will be right there in front of you.

Minor Arcana

The Eight of clubs represents continuous movement, something that is about to happen. It is the circle of life that does not stop.

Interaction between the Arcana

The major and minor arcana cards complement each other. While the mountain is static, the Eight of Clubs indicates the existence of something what moves. The challenge is great, and there are those who are content to observe the mountain from afar, but it is possible to conquer it, and this may happen soon if you act with caution.

Positive Aspects

The Mountain represents strong self-confidence and stability. Your motivation will be far greater than any difficulty you will need to overcome. This is a positive card, giving you guidance for guaranteed success if there is effort and focus on your part. Always have correct and just focus on your life so that all events will lead to your benefit. Control impulses and emotions with caution and wisdom, then you will find the best way to reach the top of this obstacle.

Negative Aspects

The downside of The Mountain is that when one fears the obstacle it prevents them from going forward, resulting in immobility. Be flexible in dealing with life's challenges, some paths may be more interesting than they seemed at first.

Work and Finances

At work, The Mountain brings great news. Changes are apparent, and you are likely to be recognized for your efforts. There is a promotion or reward on the horizon. If you want to change jobs, good news is on your way. If you are unemployed, a new challenge will come your way, and this is not bad news, this challenge is a job or an initiative that will require your attention and involvement.

The Mountain is a positive card which announces that even in the face of great challenges that can arise you must remain firm and believe in your path, you will have the strength to face the obstacles and the courage to act for your benefit. You may be going through financial problems and need to contain your spending. It is usually not the lack of money but impulsivity in spending or accomplishing goals that were not well planned. If you plan well, you will soon have some money set aside.

Love and Relationship

Single: If you are single and looking for love, do not give up. Continue your journey toward reaching the desired place with the person you are dreaming of. Fate will push you in this direction. Don't look for a perfect person, search for the person who will be right for you. Be realistic and open your heart to whoever deserves it.

In a Relationship: For those who are already in a relationship, the Mountain asks you to give your partner some more attention. It seems your focus has been heavily on material issues and your loved one is likely to be feeling left out recently. He or she needs loving care and attention.

General Aspects

Hope, perseverance, maturity, faith, strength of will, obstacles to be overcome. Confidence, security to complete a project, firmness, inclination to inflexibility, rigidity, stubbornness, difficulty to change. Truth, solidity, search, desires to be happy, facts or situations that must be evaluated rationally and practically. Good character, balance, practical side and material world. Conviction and true interests. Something or someone will bring security and support. This card announces the ideal moment to seek the achievement of a goal, especially a goal that is very important.

Message

The Mountain card advises meditation before making any decision or choice.

Card 22 – The Path

Element ~ Earth

The Path card of the Gypsy Deck is of neutral representation. That is, it needs analysis of the cards that appear in the spread alongside it to better define the direction that life is following. The Path represents our free will, our choices that will result in the construction of our being, our essence and our ways. All of us possess karmic missions that are established in our destiny, situations from which we cannot escape. How we deal with them, and the way we pursue our dreams and goals in this plane defines the whole essence of the events that will appear in the future.

When you are in doubt as to which direction to choose, analyse well what appears to have the greater reward. Look in which direction truth, wisdom, love and repetition predominate, which will certainly result in prosperity. The advice from The Path card is to not delay action, do not wait for life to pass, choose your path and fill yourself with faith and courage. You are already blessed just to be here enjoying the wonder of living, do not be afraid to be happy, even if there are some challenging moments to be overcome. Everything you plant today will be the fruit that you will reap tomorrow. Fill your path with good seeds and many flowers, which will result in joy and achievement. In health, this card asks you to be aware of your legs and feet, after all there is a long way to go and a lot of willingness and stamina is required to enjoy it.

Major Arcana

When it appears in a positive spread, The Path shows that your paths are open for moving forward and depend exclusively on the decisions made by you. Some decisions will lead you on the right track, others that will take you to a more tumultuous course. Both have the same end goal: growth, learning and happiness. A path may appear to be clean and simple, like a solid bridge built from logic and reason, but underneath run treacherous waters of emotion.

Minor Arcana

The Queen of Diamonds is very sensory and practical at the same time. She deals very well with the values of the earth, like money, sex, material possessions, and enjoys them. Love your body and enjoy the pleasures of worldly life. Preserve what is yours. This Queen has a very strong connection with physical forms and with all things that express themselves through these forms or the body.

Interaction between the Arcana

This card speaks of the free will we all have and should use. Things do not fall from the sky, we must work for them, fight for them, make the right decisions to help us get them.

Positive Aspects

When we give the Universe the best of our energy, we receive only the good in return. Even if obstacles arise, overcoming them is also a sign of evolution and wisdom. Make conscious choices, life is asking you to decide which side you want to follow, do not hesitate to live it in full.

Negative Aspects

Do not be a troublemaker, you are thirsty to live but you are not considering the effects your actions have on other people. Know that to follow your path you don't have to "trample" others. Another negative point of this card can be represented by other cards that appear in the spread, you may have made wrong choices in life which may have left you in a situation you are not happy with.

Work and Finances

The Path symbolizes success in your career, investment or professional area. You are a person who has always battled and dedicated yourself to the area in which you work, so probably good winds will come to your advantage and lead you to the recognition that you have longed for. If you are unemployed, be aware that there will be a very interesting opportunity. The Path in the Gypsy

Card suggests the promise of good things coming into your life, these will be rewards for everything you've done so far. It also asks you not to delay making decisions, embrace life with courage and everything will be well.

Love and Relationship

Single: Believe in yourself, love may be closer than you expect, so just live intensely and build your own path. Soon enough someone will come along to share that journey with you.

In a Relationship: This card presents happiness, you may be on the right path in finding peace and stability you desire, so continue to engage in the relationship without smothering each other, simply allow yourself to love and be loved with respect and trust.

General Aspects

Direction, right course, freedom of choice, goals achieved, free will, wisdom acquired from past choices and manifesting in the present. Persistence, opportunities, independence, expansion and open paths, there may be a short trip for you to take. The destiny that is written for each of us and the individual path: experiences, goals and objectives to be conquered and lived. It also symbolizes the strength of true warriors who relentlessly fight and win in their own way. The direction of the path may show the way back to your own home or could indicate the search for new horizons.

Message

Destiny, directions in life and free will.

Card 23 – The Rat

Element ~ Earth

The Rat card comes to warn about situations that if not soon resolved can create a deadlock in your life which will bring fear to continue with current projects.

This card is symbolic of an animal that is never happy with what it has, The Rat always looks for more and is a frightened creature that runs away from everything. When The Rat appears in a reading it often represents instability in our lives. You are likely to go through a testing time where you will not feel safe in any situation and you feel as though you are not able to believe in anyone.

Pay extra attention to your health, you may feel greater physical strain on your body at this time; stress with daily problems will leave you vulnerable and prone to illness.

Major Arcana
The Rat symbolizes the rodent who is never satisfied with what it has and always needs more (in every sense). Therefore, it can represent something in imbalance. This animal is seen as a multiplier of unpleasant things. They are super fertile and can bring the message of an undesirable pregnancy being on the way. The Rat is afraid of everything and does not trust anything. It symbolizes a period of trials, obstacles and wear. Although The Rat is a coward, when cornered, it turns very aggressive.

Minor Arcana
The Seven of Clubs shows that there is a test for our self-confidence and self-esteem. It also represents fear fuelled by negative external influences.

Interaction between the Arcana
Problems presented are not always resolved easily, which can lead to emotional and/or physical wear and tear on your body. This card suggests there might be some fear in facing life and problems, which is also bringing anxiety. It is good to be careful about what happens around you, especially when The Rat appears. This is a creature that sits and watches silently and tells us to beware of envy and intrigue. Remember also that rats only appear because we allow or encourage them to by leaving leftovers and rubbish. Imagine a person who is afraid of a rat but cannot set a trap. Have courage, face your problems wisely with strategies at hand, do not just run away.

Positive Aspects
Let's look at the good points of The Rat. Despite the difficulties that lie ahead, it is a very agile and smart animal. Certain cultures consider them Gods. Seek through prayers to keep yourself spirituality fortified and be as clever and skilful as The Rat. Therefore, even if this card is bringing a negative message, you will only gain a more insightful meaning when you carefully analyse everything about it. Rats do not like a clean house as there is nothing to eat.

Negative Aspects
When The Rat card comes with all its negative power, it represents the presence of dishonesty and opportunism in your life. This may come from you or from someone who will disrupt your spiritual evolution and cause very stressful times. Be very careful with the moments of stress, they will trigger spiritual and physical illnesses in you. Be careful not to have anything stolen from you; not only material goods but also your happiness. Do not let 'rats' do whatever they want in your life. Remember: the house (including your body) is yours, you are the boss.

Work and Finances
Beware that someone may be about to pull the rug out from under you. Be wise with your co-workers; do not get caught up in random gossip and stand firm on any point you know is right, there could be people just waiting for you to fail. If you are unemployed, the problem is most likely yourself. At some point in your life you have ceased to believe in yourself and your fear is apparent. You have may feel that you have become a person with no credibility because you

lack motivation. Strengthen yourself spiritually, refresh yourself with recent information from your area of expertise and everything will return to the right path. If you run your own business, do not invest in anything that does not give you a clear profit, this is not the time to waste resources. The Rat card brings you alerts for all paths of life, it is time to concentrate, reserve resources and most of all strengthen everything so that nothing from outside can bring damage to your life. Pay attention to where money is being spent without real need. Do not be compulsive and beware of discouragement. If you are aware of the problems, you will be able to solve everything soon.

Love and Relationship

Single: If you are single this card advises you to analyse recent relationships well to see if the problem is really the others or if it is in fact you.

In a Relationship: The Rat in love symbolizes presence of friction in the relationship, so try not to feed the negative energy. Be very careful with third parties, as The Rat suggests that someone may try to steal what is yours and lead to your unhappiness. This card appearing is not a certain indication that there is a betrayal, but rather reminds you of the need to communicate more so that there is no weak spot. This makes it harder for other people to find a way to weaken the bond between the two of you.

General Aspects

Loss of energy and/or material objects, theft, characteristics of negative energies, greed, discouragement, annoyance, weariness, influence, negativity, need for spiritual cleansing, aggression that hides insecurity, assaults, malaise, a message of warning about enemies which harm us in some way. Disease, lack of vitality, vampirism, impotence and sadness, forgetfulness, cheating, malice, disorder and unbalance. Opportunistic people who come to take advantage despite the chance of hurting someone. Warns about the danger of illicit business, misery (emotional, mental, physical and/or spiritual).

Message

Integrity and the strength of spirit are the only ways to overcome the adversities announced by this card.

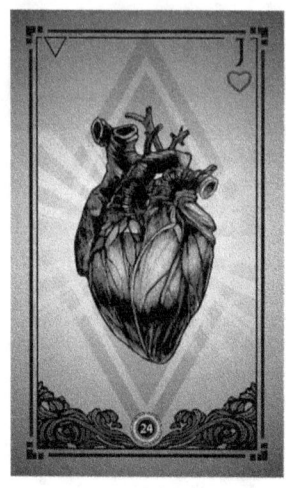

Card 24 – The Heart

Element – Water

The Heart appears in the Gypsy Deck as card number 24. Its meaning is the purest love. Love where one owes nothing and does not expect anything in return; love which does not need to support the other person, but which feeds the growth together. It expresses the most delicate harmony of beneficial giving in exchange for feelings and wisdom between two people or between the main areas in focus.

It is very difficult for humans to understand the true meaning of love. Sometimes we plunge into a deep sense of passion and believe it is love, but the essence of love and passion are quite different. The genuine love that The Heart in the Gypsy Deck shows is that which begins in self-love, for only those who love themselves first can love their companion. This feeling, when it reaches the level of its ultimate essence, conveys peace and tranquillity. A true love does not demand, it does not lean on the other for support, it holds hands and walks at the same pace. Thus, The Heart, one of the most beautiful cards in this deck, wants to convey a deep sense of pleasure and sincerity in all matters of life. This is the phase when you are likely to feel fulfilled and satisfied with everything that is happening in your life. The Heart card promises wonders and achievements in your life.

Major Arcana
There is no card more beautiful than this! The Heart is the best representation of love. This is where we feel the sense of security and joy, what shows our affectionate and sentimental side.

Minor Arcana
The Jack of Hearts is a loving, sensitive and emotional young man. He is the man in love, willing to do anything to make his beloved happy with no expectation of receiving anything in return.

Interaction between the Arcana
Genuiness of love is being put to test. First, self-love, then love to/from another person, work, even pets or dedication to a greater cause. Decisions are made with joy and there is satisfaction in everything that you do. There is a lot of surrender and acceptance. Many good things are on the way and there is no doubt that there is happiness around and within you.

Positive Aspects
This is the time to expect to see the benefits of everything you have been striving to achieve. Whether it is work, studies, love relationship, friendship, family or any other dream, this moment is conducive of putting your love into everything you do, and in return The Heart promises great rewards. Serenity, delicacy and appreciation, only those who truly love themselves and life will know how to take advantage of this unique moment without getting lost, without straying from the right path and enjoying every little gift that will arrive at this stage. Put this essence of surrender, happiness and sincere rewards into whatever your question is, and you will find the direction in which The Heart wants to guide you.

Negative Aspects
Not everything we receive is good if there is no balance. Therefore, The Heart asks you to take good care of it and remember that everything in exaggeration only brings sorrows. Be careful not to be overbearing with your love, do not put anyone in a pedestal, do not put all of your focus on one type of love. You must not forget that companionship and dedication to others is important to progress in life. Also, be cautious that you don't over-commit yourself, so you forget your dreams and live the plans of others instead. Make sure your love is unconditional and that there is no co-dependency or excess of attraction.

Work and Finances
This is a great time to give your heart to the profession you love. In the Gypsy Deck, The Heart says that you will succeed if you follow what gives you pleasure in work. Bet on happiness, and achievements will come soon! If you are unemployed it is time to take a risk, go and apply for that job you always dreamt of enthusiastically. Dedicate your time and willingness only to what promises to make you a happy person altogether. With a message as beautiful as the picture, the Heart in the Gypsy Deck is a pure card that brings a message of evolution to everything done with love, tranquillity and integrity.

Love and Relationship
Single: Let the heart speak louder, throw the grudges away, and enjoy the love that life will soon give you as a gift. The Heart certainly suggests that you are about to live a great love. For this, one must also surrender, both in body and soul.

In a Relationship: The Heart card tells you that you should not be afraid. Give yourself completely to the person you love. There is no chance of betrayal and this will probably be one of the most beautiful experiences between the two of you. Everything will happen perfectly, and you will be in tune with one another. So, give your love freely and allow yourself to be loved in return. Do not cling to the number of anniversaries, let the feeling flow regardless of whether you have been together for 30 years or one day. Do not be suspicious.

General Aspects
Feelings, emotions, dedication, desire, surrender, human warmth, the treasures in our hearts, intuitive attitudes, the voice of the heart, emotional balance, sensitivity, truth, sincerity and transparency. This card reminds us that the heart must be the abode of noble feelings, unconditional love, full joy and happiness.

Message
This card never defines, but intensifies, enlivens and highlights situations pointed out by other cards.

Card 25 – The Ring

Element ~ Water

The Ring, sometimes known as The Alliance, is card 25 of the Gypsy Deck. It symbolizes commitment to something or someone, a strong bond that fills our chest with good hopes. This is a positive card which says that you should put all your plans and most intimate dreams into practice. It is important to remember that for everything to work out, you will need an alliance, someone very special and trustworthy that will give you the feeling of security and will allow you to follow the path you have long sought throughout your life.

Tighten your bonds with the most interesting people and they will guarantee you a good future, believe in the possibilities and allow joy to encourage you in everything that is new and necessary to complete the transformation of your path. Remembering that The Ring doesn't only represent love relationships, but also any type of partnership and involvement that allows the realization of a dream - be it financial, professional, loving or any other area.

Major Arcana
This is a card that many people would be happy to see in a reading. It is understandable, The Ring symbolizes the union and alliance of two people, whether in the field of friendship, love, work or even spirituality. It reflects commitment to someone or to a cause. Whenever this card comes out, the first meaning is union.

Minor Arcana
The Ace of Clubs is one of the symbols of fire. Its meaning represents fruitfulness, prosperity and abundance. The card symbolizes the beginning of new ventures, a start of possible innovations. The Ace of Clubs also represents transformations, life force and energy that governs the world.

Interaction between the Arcana
Communion, the beginning of a good and committed union. Things are done with love and loyalty. The Ring always brings a message of optimism and happiness. It is the time to put dreams into practice, always together with someone else.

Positive Aspects
The Ring brings the news of happiness through realization of projects. To achieve this dream, you will have the help of someone dearly loved who will influence you to the point of putting you on the right path to your achievements. In health it indicates a good phase, but menopausal women need to seek their feminine essence so as not to become emotionally unbalanced. If you are waiting for the arrival of a little angel, know it is the perfect moment for the realization of this plan; the energies will be in favour.

Negative Aspects
The negative side of The Ring card suggests failure to pursue dreams due to personal isolation, or breakup of a partnership. For this obstacle to occur, the other cards in the spread must show this path.

Work and Finances
The Ring brings a message of good fruits gathered mainly as a team. You will find the support needed to progress your plans from your co-workers. Companionship will be the key to success. If you have your own business, take a good look at the opportunities that will arise from partnerships, they can pay off.

Love and Relationship
Single: The Ring indicates a possible surrounding passion that will fill you with security. This is likely to be the time when you meet someone who will make you feel happy to commit, someone you can trust due to the energy they show you.

In a Relationship: If you already have a partner, know that there is a great deal of loyalty in this union, so there is no need to have any thoughts of mistrust. Instead, work together with your partner and share each other's strengths as you continue your projects and enjoy personal achievements.

General Aspects

Marriage, equality, love, society, sincerity, positive spiritual bonds, need to hold hands, courtship, partnerships, group projects, help, spiritual bond, new friendships, good people around us. The harmony of sharing our lives and our paths with someone. Cooperation, support and fraternity. It can also indicate encounter between soulmates.

Message

Invitations to commit, trust, give and receive, help in the pursuit of the same ideal.

Card 26 – The Book

Element ~ Air

The Book is card 26 and it symbolizes achievements through understanding. Books are a source of wisdom that need interpretation to be fully absorbed and understood; so only the deepest study and analysis can define the best directives of life. When this card was created, the people in society who had access to reading and documents were privileged, so when The Book appears in a reading, it suggests this is a time of growth and privilege by being empowered to acquire wisdom in your life.

This card has a positive meaning if you are willing to accept new points of view and extract your greatest strengths and learning from each stage of your life. Destiny is giving you the possibility of choices and putting tools into your hands that serve precisely to increase your ability to discern and analyse the opportunities and facts in question. It is as if you have a knife in one hand and cheese in the other, what you do depends only on your analysis and decision.

Major Arcana
Remember, the Gypsy Deck was originally created in the 18th century, when not everyone had access to the books and being able to read them was a privilege. However, with effort it was possible to understand its content. Each book brings a teaching that will undoubtedly help your inner growth.

Minor Arcana

The Ten of Diamonds represents prosperity that always flows. It is a representation of the expected completion of a cycle, achievement of an established goal. For everything to happen the way we want, it takes work and dedication.

Interaction between the Arcana

The Book represents not only knowledge but learning that can exist in all situations. It's up to us to put it into practice. Do not be fooled into thinking you already know everything. There is always something new to be learned and skills can be improved. By doing this, everything that has been planted will be harvested, with great certainty. This is a card that calls for discipline, respect, and reflection. When this card relates to a person, they usually appear serious, like a closed book.

Positive Aspects

This arcane symbolizes knowledge, where the phases of life are sources of inspiration and learning in your path. These have made you wiser, more determined to make good choices and set the best guidelines. Success is imminent and will happen if you are willing to pursue that goal. Keep in mind that to reach the point you want you will need to put in the effort required. Your mind is ready to set the guidelines, but you must also act. Do not waste time!

Negative Aspects

Nobody will ever know everything in one lifetime. Make no mistake that your experiences were enough for a lifetime, knowledge has no limits and it is changeable. People change their opinions all the time and this also changes the flow of life and society. Do not deceive yourself by being too proud to the point of not accepting other visions of world and life. There is always something new that we can learn or improve, so do not dwell only on scenarios you have already witnessed and on beliefs that do not allow your thoughts to be evolutionary.

Work and Finances

You are someone who always looks calmly and wisely for a solutions to possible problems. However, you may appear to be unapproachable, which can mean you are sometimes a little feared by co-workers; although everyone knows that you are trustworthy. Continue to focus on what you want to accomplish so that fruits will be harvested in the future because you deserve it. If you are unemployed this card warns you to pay more attention to your goals, it is important for you to focus right now. No matter how complicated the time is, you need to clearly identify with what it is that you want to do and go deeper into your studies. In this way, you will be able to portray yourself as someone who really understands the profession you want to pursue. The Book indicates good news for those who dedicate themselves to what they like and dream about. It is the announcement that good results will come forth in the future if you really devote yourself to what you want to achieve.

Love and Relationship

Single: You are likely to be someone who is tired of living illusions so you are careful in choosing the next person to whom you will relate, this is not bad! This card does not predict someone's immediate arrival, but states that when you meet this special person, they will be someone very striking and with ideals very similar to yours, which will cause a great affinity between the two of you.

In a Relationship: The Book indicates that your relationship is one of extreme fidelity and companionship. The important thing at this time is to pay attention to romanticism and communication and you'll have everything you need to succeed. Be more dedicated to paying attention to each other and expressing your love and affection. Even if we know when we are loved, it is nice to hear it spoken out loud. If by chance you have recently separated, this card represents the real decision of what is happening, the story is over, the book is closed and at this moment there is no chance of a return. If it is not you who chose the separation, it is important that you work on your self-esteem before seeking another person's love.

General Aspects

Analysis, intelligence, need to study, think before making decisions. Wisdom is acquired through the many paths that life offers. Intellectual effort, work, solutions are reached with the mind and reasoning. It can represent the workplace or studies, papers, documents, bureaucracy and legal matters. It is an invitation to reflect on possibilities and analyse both sides of any situation. Gathering, wisdom, maturity and serenity, need for specialization or improvement in something.

Message

The announcement of self-development through culture and intellectual potentials.

Card 27 – The Letter

Element ~ ALL

In the Gypsy Deck, card 27 is The Letter and it brings news! When it is not accompanied by a negative card, it will only bring good news, and it may be by any means of communication. Who knows, perhaps a long-awaited love will come, or the desired job. It suggests a moment of justice. After much ordeal, an expected positive response will finally emerge. You can receive interesting invitations or some friendly messages at a very important time in your life.

Get ready to receive the revelations you need, they will come soon. Pending issues can be resolved, issues that have troubled you will be finalized; a new phase will arise and new paths will appear. Be prepared to accept the new. Like every message, it can bring a warning on a sensitive subject the emergence of which you may not have noticed yet. It is essential that you keep secrets others share with you, someone may seek to vent something very intimate with you. It is important that this information is not shared with others, else you risk losing the trust of your friend.

Major Arcana
The number 27 is associated with The Hermit from the Major Arcana of the Tarot. The image that The Letter seeks to highlight is that of the message that arrives. It is usually represented very simply, with the image of a letter, sometimes brought by a white dove. The Letter itself is a neutral card, neither positive nor negative. Look at the other cards in the spread to indicate its characteristics, which can change depending on what it is surrounded by.

Minor Arcana

The Spades suit is associated with the Air element: exchange of ideas, conflicts and rapid changes. The Seven of Spades indicates that you have new plans to fulfil but may have to face difficulties due to interference from other people. It is a warning about the existence of blockages in our life and a possibility of hidden enemies who are interfering with your plans. It indicates that someone may be hiding the truth from you, or that you yourself are not admitting what you really feel or desire.

Interaction between the Arcana

The Letter initially reveals that you will receive an important message, or a revelation will be made. Whether this message is positive or negative is only revealed by the other cards in the spread. We can say that the revelation of this message is fundamental for the higher good of your development. It is important to remember that it is a card that speaks of the present moment and not of the future. This message can be received by any of the vast means of communication that we have today: email, text message, phone call, or a traditional letter in the mail. It suggests that we should analyse the words of the message ourselves to get the deeper meaning, rather than talk about it which can negatively influence the progress of plans.

Positive Aspects

The contents of this card can have great news! You may get a message you have been waiting for, or a solution to a problem that was causing sleepless nights. It is very important that regardless of what it is, to be discreet and not just tell everyone about it. You never know who can pull the rug out from under your feet before the goal is completed. Be patient, and even if you are excited to share the subject wait until everything is confirmed and has become a reality. New opportunities will arise, be open to new challenges, new plans and paths. Don't be afraid, this is what you have been waiting for all this time! Arm yourself with faith and courage and start your new journey on the right foot.

Negative Aspects

Not all the messages we receive are the ones we expected. Bad news may also come when this card appears. Be prepared to understand this and turn into opportunities or learnings that will always be positive in the end. It will leave you stronger and smarter, with more ability to overcome obstacles. If someone looks for you to tell you a secret, listen but keep your mouth shut, do not tell anyone else. If you spread it you may be the one to suffer the consequences and guilt will fall all over you. So, if the central theme is not something that involves you and depends solely on your decision, do not take sides, do not embrace the subject, as the result could be someone taking offense or hurting your life.

Work and Finances

Have you been long waiting for that promotion or salary increase? The Letter appears to let you know that someone will give you this good news soon. If you are unemployed, that confirmation message of a new job is on the way! Just remember, whether the message is positive or not, keep it secret, in a work environment especially it is very important to maintain discretion. In the Gypsy Deck, The Letter can mean different types of messages, but the main thing is that you are aware of the secrets, be discreet and do not spread them and regardless of what news The Letter brings new paths will emerge and you will have new options in front of you.

Love and Relationship

Single: The Letter can mean the confession of a desire or a proposal of dating someone. Hidden feelings are about to be revealed, something you don't yet know. Be prepared to feel your heart soar because this card promises happiness.

In a Relationship: Someone's most hidden feelings will be revealed, and they will envelop you! In a surprising way a person can come into your life with a message of love. The Letter suggests an even more serious step in the relationship.

General Aspects

Alert, warning to take care, writing, attention and messages. Communication, dialogue, situations that need to be grasped quickly, intensifies the meaning of other cards around it.

Message

Divine blessings, surprises and revelations.

Card 28 – The Gypsy Man

Element ~ Earth

This is Card 28, The Gypsy Man. Of neutral representation, its interpretation is based on the other combinations that will appear in the spread. The Gypsy figure alone is a symbol of resistance to the persecutions that these nomadic people faced in the history of their journey. Even in the face of adversity they maintain their position, preserve their culture and do not lose the joy of living. The energy of this card is masculine, so its symbol is focused on an action that will be influenced by an important figure of this gender. If you are a man, this message is about yourself, and if you are a woman, it is a male person that will mark this moment in your life.

The Gypsy Man is a logical card; therefore, it suggests an idea that will be realized or that there will be a strong will to find a way or a solution to a problem. Emotions can be put aside at this stage. If put to a test, when a Gypsy has the knowledge of what is best for him and those around him, he will act without question, even if it is not what he desires. His actions will be what he deems to be fairest for all. In health, beware of tension and remember that this card can represent a special male in your life; he can be a son, father or partner who will do anything to ensure your happiness or protection. He does so because he feels that this is his obligation in life.

Major Arcana

The Gypsy Man appears as a symbolic representation of nomadic and free-spirited men, often persecuted, but still able to follow their cultural traditions; keeping their work, their joy, and defending their families. The number 28 is associated with the Magician, Major Arcanum of the Tarot. The image of the Gypsy Man seeks to highlight confidence. Generally, he is represented in a quite imposing form, always well dressed and adorned with jewels, representing his success. It is a card of the Gypsy Deck that also represents masculine energy, with both positive and negative aspects. For whoever the Gypsy Man is, he is on the move and is a very determined person; manly, courageous and knows how to use reason to achieve his goals.

Minor Arcana

The Ace of Hearts reflects everything that the heart desires - a happy family, true and harmonious friends, passionate lovers and a peace of mind. You are likely to be surrounded by great solidarity that can be used in any area of life. This card brings balance to materialistic situations and extinguishes concerns. On the negative side, it can tear the heart in love and brings general restlessness.

Interaction between the Arcana

The Gypsy Man represents the masculine principle, active, positive, Yang, rational thinking. It does represent a male figure. Again, if you are a woman, this card represents an influential man in your life - father, husband, lover or perhaps your boss. Psychologically it is associated with differentiating and ordering, representing the will, power, actions and logic. The Gypsy Man is he who, though he loves, makes reason prevail. He is very articulate, but also has the will, strength and courage to act when necessary and doesn't rely on his intellect alone.

Positive Aspects

Courage, protection, disposition, agile and rational thinking. It is time to do everything wisely and honestly to bring the best, not only for you, but for all of your loved ones. If you were going through a moment of fear and doubt, know that this will be the trigger of encouragement you needed to stop delaying something important. This card brings the ambition to compete and the energy to win.

Negative Aspects

When the male energy is not well applied it can generate scattered thoughts and sudden changes without fundamental actions, which will cause more confusion in your life than bliss. This card also brings a health alert, stay in tune with your body and visit a doctor to find out if everything is well, do not neglect important issues. Testosterone, male hormone essential for human life has its adversities, like acting without thinking, fighting without reason, arduous sexual desire, aggressive attitudes, creepy and predatory side.

Work and Finances

Do not let inconsistency disrupt your evolution at work, use your courage and creativity to direct your attention to important issues that will ensure your good image prevails in your work. Your commitment and dedication to what is a priority will bring you the highlight deserved by your effort. The Gypsy Man card brings strength and willingness to perform tasks that are important yet often remain pending in our lives. A male figure will be the main piece in this moment of transition.

Love and Relationship

Single: If you are a heterosexual woman, The Gypsy Man card indicates the beginning of a romance, if you are a heterosexual man indicates the need to seek the masculine elements of your nature. In case of LGBTIQ someone with masculine energy stronger than yours is likely to appear.

In a Relationship: It is a time of full confidence, where reason will create the most concrete and secure base of the relationship. Your ideas for deepening the relationship will be more grounded as they will have a more realistic analysis of what really matters to you both. Enjoy the moments next to the one you love and always remember that relationship is about equality; do not forget to listen to what is important for your partner.

General Aspects

Power, mastery, invocation, action, possession, realization, firmness, execution, decision and maturity, high confidence and structure. The provider.
He always represents a figure of power, such as father, husband, companion, son, boss, and friend, a man of power or even you. There is also a possibility of indicating the masculine side, which we all possess regardless of gender. Stability, authority, jealousy, reason, strength, commitment and dedication. Hard work, conquest, obstinacy and courage.

Message

Dominance and power.

Card 29 – The Gypsy Woman

Element ~ Water

Card 29 of the Gypsy Deck is The Gypsy Woman, and it brings in its essence all the Yin energy i.e. the female characteristics. This card symbolizes female power, so it can be a woman that will influence your life or can be you if you are female. In its most primal symbolism, the one that came from the gypsy people, this card is the concept of force in femininity. These women have accepted the challenge of facing fate and the road of life in search of wisdom and are so free and determined that they act as their hearts lead them.

Its energy in the Gypsy Deck is quite neutral and the reading will depend on the other cards in the spread. Therefore, whether this woman will represent good or bad will depend on the whole context expressed in the reading. What is important to be aware of is that this female figure knows very well what she wants and how to get it. She is the expression of courage, seduction and intellectual strength. In health, this card calls for care to avoid times of stress that can tear you down both physically and emotionally.

Major Arcana
The Gypsy Woman appears as a symbolic representation of nomadic and free-spirited women, often persecuted, but still able to follow their cultural traditions, maintaining her beauty, joy, and forming a family. The number 29 is

associated with The High Priestess from the Major Arcanum of the Tarot. The image of The Gypsy Woman seeks to highlight the beauty and mystery of those who know the occult and is usually portrayed quite imposingly, showing a woman who knows the gifts she possesses and how to use them to get what she wants.

Minor Arcana

Quite often cards with the air element carry a message of loss, but the Ace of Spades is a positive card. It says that in your mind you have everything you need to achieve success; just put your plans into action. You may lack motivation and courage right now, but you must act. Don't hold on to anything that weighs you down, simply let go of what is causing problems and this will be your solution. If you are uncertain about what the actual problem is you could at least notice the feeling of something holding you back. Know that soon you'll be able to see the path, and when that happens you will need the determination to act.

Interaction between the Arcana

This is a card that also represents the feminine in its positive and negative aspects. For whoever the Gypsy Woman on the move is, she is a very determined person who knows her value and fights for what she wants. She is willing to use everything that the Sacred Feminine gives her in order to reach her goal. We are talking about strength through words, subtlety, affection, docile gestures and kindness. The Gypsy Woman is like water that slowly pierces a stone without the stone realizing it. It is unwise to provoke her wrath. One of her negative points is inconstancy and all her kindness can turn into fury if something, or especially someone dear to her, is put at risk.

Positive Aspects

Either yourself (if you are a woman), or a female close to you is a strong person who fights for everything that she wants. This woman has a great deal of energy and is full of determination and mysteries. It is never known just how she will act, but you can be certain she will do everything possible to achieve success in life. Nobody can call her weak, because life has presented her with many challenges and yet she is still strong. As much as emotions sometimes rock The Gypsy Woman, her ability to overcome obstacles and keep on chasing her dreams in the pursuit of happiness excels despite anything. She has a unique ability to multi-task and give unconditional love, with a natural gift at motherhood. When she chooses not to, or cannot have children, she often adopts children or pets, or seeks another way to explore her caring and nurturing side.

Negative Aspects
Do not be passive and don't allow others to make life decisions for you. Let go of everything that causes you pain and suffering. You may be emotional, but you still possess the ability to be happy. If you are a man this card indicates that a striking woman is dominating your life or will do soon. Be careful as she may lead you on paths that are only in her best interests! In all aspects, do not let emotional instability consume you, be more attentive and do not leave projects unfinished. Due to hormonal imbalance, the negative characteristics are inconstancy, occultism, secrecy and anxiety.

Work and Finances
Avoid disruptions at work, do not get involved in gossip and don't get caught up in emotional issues. A woman can help you completely change your life. If a good opportunity arises then grab it, but if there is a female at work that seems to be negative, avoid contact with her as much as possible. If you are unemployed, a good position is likely to be offered by a woman who stands out; invest time in making contact with such women. The essential thing to know is that your emotions are likely to be highlighted at this time and the will to fight for what you believe will become even more pronounced.

Love and Relationship
Single: You are likely to meet someone around this time who will fascinate you. Take care not to get involved with people who are not worth your time though, as you'll only end up getting hurt later!

In a Relationship: The woman in the relationship will be looking to shower her partner with a lot of love and sensuality. This card indicates female power acting on the couple, enjoy and reap unforgettable moments for both. If you do not have a very good connection, be aware that an unwanted female may come into your life, offering opinions you don't want to hear, or even a new passion.

General Aspects
Intuition, feeling, trust, sense, ambition, creativity, emotions, security, power of decision, optimism, responsibility, generosity. Good intentions, life and renewal. It can represent a mother, daughter, sister, wife or boss, other powerful women or these characteristics in you. It can also mean rise of our feminine side that everyone has, regardless of gender.

Message
Maternity, love, intuition and trust.

Card 30 – The Lily

Element ~ Water

This is card number 30 of the Gypsy Deck. The Lily comes with an energy full of delicacy, promises of good times, sincerity, eternal love and prosperity. This card represents a time of discovery of your true power, of your essence, something you never thought you could possess. Achieving your dreams and goals will be easier, simply because you want to and will fight with much confidence and love for it. These flowers convey the purity of a desire, and in the same way you will deal with details to organize and structure your life. The lily must grow and convey its grace, so will your soul, full of happiness and longing to walk the most beautiful paths that will bring you true happiness. Stay focused and calm and let the lilies blossom on your path as they promise that a period of good times is coming.

Major Arcana
Lilies are beautiful flowers that delight in delicacy and candour. They are very popular in wedding bouquets. It is one of the most famous flowers of Feng Shui and in this tradition it represents summer, abundance, eternal love and purity.

Minor Arcana
The King of Spades represents a man of great wisdom and uses his intellectual knowledge to solve any problems. During the Middle Ages, this king was associated with King David, a wise Jewish strategist who freed his people and ruled around 1050 BC.

Interaction between the Arcana

The Lily card represents the union between the internal powers that we often do not even realise we have. Each personal achievement requires determination, dedication and this happens because you want to grow and achieve a planned goal. The presence of this card in a reading announces that your determination has not been in vain, your objectives will be fulfilled. Stay calm as your goals will be achieved with balance and tranquillity.

Positive Aspects

This is a very positive card, promising that you will fulfil your dreams, for the lilies' bloom is the result of all that was planted in the course of life. It is a pure and beautiful harvest of the efforts and good energies that you have employed so far. Nothing happens at random, everything is the result of past actions. Receive these flowers with all the joy in the world, do not cover yourself and try to accelerate the process. Admire your achievements with wisdom and satisfaction for all the good you have done in your life. Make the most of happiness.

Negative Aspects

The Lily does not have a negative message, in fact it softens any negativity. For instance, if The Lily were to appear in a spread where there is a separation between a couple, it would indicate that there is something generating some disharmony between them. There is an issue that can be simply solved by delicately analysing. The presence of The Lily would suggest that nothing worse is likely.

Work and Finances

You are in a period of high spirituality, tranquillity and certainty of the direction you have chosen. That energy will attract people's attention. Employee, unemployed or owner of your own business - The Lily is a sign of achievement and success through good relationships with people. Enjoy this unique power of understanding yourself in the best way with others and with yourself. Take some quiet time out for yourself and look within before making decisions. The Lily card conveys the promise of achievements; they will be the fruit of your commitment throughout your life, so know that you deserve happiness on this path full of flowers, enjoy it.

Love and Relationship

Single: If you are single and living in fear of a new relationship (even though you want company very much), stay tuned, you'll be forced out of your comfort zone because someone very attractive will come your way. Allow yourself to evolve and take the risk again, give yourself to love.

In a Relationship: For those who are married this card indicates a stable union, even if there is some "bickering". You know how to understand and forgive, because you cannot imagine being distant from your partner. There is balance and a lot of love in the relationship. For those who are engaged or dating, you have a beautiful story ahead, with great chances of this being the true "forever together". Remember to respect the space of your partner and let them go out and spend time with friends; you don't have to spend every waking moment together.

General Aspects
Balance, protection, harmony, detachment, happiness, self-knowledge, purpose of soul, tranquillity, serenity, warmth, truth, euphoria, well-being, peace, the desires of the soul and the discovery of self. Happy period, end of crises and new perspectives. At times it symbolizes intuition and spiritual life in tune with the Universe. Spontaneity and innocence.

Message
The Lily is always a positive sign of good energy coming; announces prosperity.

Card 31 – The Sun
Element ~ Fire

You are in a moment of recovery and The Sun, card 31 of the Gypsy Deck, brings you promise of growth, prosperity and victory. This positive card presents the beginning of good moments that will bring success in life. The power of logical reasoning and analysis of the facts will allow you to take advantage of the best opportunities that will cross your path. So, enjoy this enlightening and focused mindset to build the foundations of your dreams; your most anticipated projects. If you have been waiting for the right moment, know that now is a great time to put plans into practice.

Do not be afraid to live and let yourself be carried by The Sun, for it promises to shine a lot of light on your path. Your enlightenment will lead you along the best road, without resentments, fears and yearnings. This card also symbolizes fertility, so if you are considering parenthood, this may be your time.

Major Arcana
The Sun has been a strong symbol since the earliest civilizations. Always possessing a positive aspect, it represented the light of the day, which freed the people from the darkness of the night. In this sense, The Sun was a God. Widely studied, other meanings were added as humanity began to understand more about what the Sun really was. The number 31 is associated with The Emperor, Major Arcanum of the Tarot. The image of the Sun seeks to highlight its exuberant yellow and its powerful rays. It is usually represented in this colour in order to relate to wealth.

Minor Arcana

Ace of Diamonds indicates that it is time to put into practice the most daring plans, the ones you have always been afraid to risk. However, always use reasoning and understand why, to get more foundation to support your ideas. Understand that everything will come to fruition as long as it is not something played as the wind blows and without plans. If you allow yourself to be ambitious on the path of success, everything indicates that luck is on your side and the period is favourable to reap the best fruits. Be objective and analyse the general context of your life so that you can immediately put into practice everything you can before this phase passes.

Interaction between the Arcana

The Sun card indirectly reveals emergence of competition and disputes. But, you have nothing to worry about since the sun *will* shine, and you will be the reaper of success. It reveals a competitive person, who likes to mark their presence and win the battles that he/she is willing to face. This card suggests that victory is certain, and there is nothing to fear. The Sun's brightness will dazzle your opponents and will light your way. However, knowing how to choose your battles is a sign of true magnificence. Remember that too much sun burns instead of just bringing light. Shine your light where necessary and be certain that you use your intelligence and aptitude in a way that ensures everything has the best foundations. If your steps and objectives are well planned, be sure that you can act with confidence that everything will happen in the best way possible.

Positive Aspects

Promise has come to solve all the problems that haunted you so far. With the brightness of The Sun, you will be able to rebuild and have the necessary disposition to invest in your projects. This time, your attitude will be more logical and well-researched before you act, as this card promises better clarity and a broader view of life.

Negative Aspects

At the same time as The Sun illuminates, it can also burn. Therefore, depending on the other cards of the reading, this period may be surrounded by excesses, where some events can destroy everything that seemed like a perfect road for you. Be aware of all signs that life gives and do not take risks if something does not feel right for you. Do not let scorching sun catch you in the middle of the road.

Work and Finances
Your vitality and positive energy will radiate a lot of credibility about you to your superiors. This can give you growth in your professional environment. Have strength and focus, knowing that you are on the road to success and accomplishments. If you are unemployed, The Sun's energy will increase your personal brilliance. Use your creativity to find the best outlets if market is crowded, because this card will highlight you. The Sun appears in the Gypsy Deck full of life and promises favourable events, for it is the main energy that feeds the life force and guides toward achievements and success.

Love and Relationship
Single: Your power of seduction shows in the glow of your skin at this time, you will be able to enchant the person you desire. Be careful not to get hurt with temporary involvements, choose your prospective partner well if you are looking for something more solid and long-lasting.

In a Relationship: It is a perfect time for the couple to show how much they love each other. Their bodies are filled with the warmth of The Sun's hot energy and it will help you if you have recently been lacking signs of love. Therefore, enjoy and love your partner intensely; giving yourself to them is what is needed for this period, it will give you greater involvement and closeness with your partner.

General Aspects
Prosperity, light, victory, self-affirmation, happy moments, intelligence, vital energy, marriage, union, society, creative force, power, growth, purpose of souls, expansion, beneficent energies, personal brilliance, wisdom, truth, the soul, clarity, consciousness, harmony, recognition, meeting of twin souls. Courage and inner power. It can represent the father or a male figure; self-knowledge, inner ascension, joys, success, realization, active intelligence, completeness, expansion, birth and progress.

Message
Favourable moments in all aspects.

Card 32 – The Moon
Element ~ Water

The Moon, card 32 in the Gypsy Deck, suggests energy and inspiration for the most passionate. The Moon seduces and envelops and is a symbol of deeper relationships. The Moon indicates strong feelings, those that can make us shiver from head to toes. We cannot forget that the shadow and the night can also bring a feeling of uncertainty, mystery and mistrust, which can make it seem more attractive to focus on the limits in life and believe we can avoid suffering by not trying to live beyond those limits. It is far better to create a balance, don't hide from the possibilities that may arise, it is okay to allow your emotions to flow through you, but limit them so that they don't become overwhelming. Don't let one pleasurable situation become the only happiness in your life. Remember that the joy of living is in balance, both in your life and in who you are.

Major Arcana
The Moon represents the romantic side of lovers and poets. However, this card can bring us a feeling that there is something hidden. It is wise to take a step back and be aware of what is real and what is an illusion. When The Moon appears in a reading, it indicates that emotions are in full bloom and at the same time care must be taken not to hide those feelings.

Minor Arcana
The Eight of Hearts announces the possibility of a romance or the fulfilment of a relationship. Despite all the romanticism, one must be aware of the challenge of balancing imagination with real life.

Interaction between the Arcana
If other cards in the reading are positive, The Moon suggests that you will find the answers you seek by using your own intuition. Balance will happen smoothly when the mind and heart are open to hear each other. Beware of seeking an escape from reality and substance abuse.

Positive Aspects
In the Gypsy Deck, The Moon is a very complex card to read, because it is so connected to the energy of the other cards that will come out in the spread. When associated with a positive message, it symbolizes a strong intuitive power that will guide the person to the necessary conclusions in their life. Your spirit will be inspired and will guide strength to your heart and mind, balancing both. This wisdom will bring you the expected benefits, diminishing everything that causes you suffering or makes you restless.

Negative Aspects
When The Moon appears with negative cards in a reading, the message can be that the fear of being hurt is making it impossible for you to fully live the good moments of life. It can also be a warning that you may end up not loving yourself while you are living illusively and depend on another person. This can lead to depression if the situation or relationship does not last or evolve as you hope.

Work and Finances
You are someone with mysterious energy and quite likely get very involved and devote a great deal of energy to your work. Because of your dedication, you become very skilled at what you do and are consequently envied by your peers. Keep your eyes open for self-interested people, they may be craving your position. Stay away from unnecessary gossip and do not comment too much on activities that are non-work related. These attitudes will help you protect yourself. If you have your own business, focus on the interesting investment opportunities that will come, this is a good time to grow. If you are unemployed, get moving now, do not be lamenting - this card indicates that you will find

what you are looking for and deserve. Although you may still have a short distance to go on your road, good opportunities will come, do not stand still!

The Moon indicates depth in emotions and relationships of all types, which can bring illusion and surrender. Use your intuitive power and your wisdom to take advantage of this good immersion energy. Balance is the key word for this moment, it will bring harmony and success into your life. Although this card is positive regarding finances, it is important that you don't spend more than necessary at this time.

Love and Relationship

Single: Know that someone striking is likely to cross your path. Free yourself from the shackles of past sufferings that keep you from risking your happiness again. There is a great chance that this person is from a different culture than yours, they may follow a different religion or philosophies.

In a Relationship: The Moon in love indicates giving between the couple. If you are dating or engaged, marriage is likely to come soon. If you are married, this card indicates that there is love and surrender, but it is necessary that you expose deeper or hidden feelings to rejuvenate the relationship. If there has been trouble in the relationship, The Moon shows great love on the part of the partner. Maybe it is time to talk sincerely and see if there is a chance to reconcile your differences.

General Aspects

Recognition ofs values, sensibility, intuition, dreams, desires, fantasies, honours, changes, intuition, faith, power of magic and influences of the astral plane. Hidden feelings, inner mazes. In a subtler sense, it may indicate a troubled emotional life and past situations that need to be resolved in the present. It can suggest the influence of a female figure in your life, a powerful woman who acted as the catalyst for changes. It may mean that a secret, something hidden is about to be revealed. It brings the fear of the future, inner darkness, emotional confusion and instability.

Message

Be prepared for changes, be flexible and try to adapt.

Card 33 – The Key
Element ~ Earth

The Key in the Gypsy Deck appears in a reading to open doors with the solutions needed in your life. All barriers will be destroyed and overcome. You simply need to have the focus and willpower to proceed. The Key will give you the opportunity to succeed in your goals and your success will depend on your commitment to make it happen. You will have the tools in your hands, so believe in your ideas and your decision-making power. You are experiencing an enlightened moment, and everything will be in the best possible way, do not doubt it.

You will be on the road to success, and this can unfortunately attract the attention of envious and negative people. Be careful not to entrust your plans and secrets to people you do not know well, they may not have your best interest in mind. Remember, sometimes appearances can deceive. In the financial arena, The Key symbolizes the arrival of money, success and prosperity. However, there will also be new possibilities for discoveries and horizons to be explored, which will require much attention and use of everything new that you will experience.

Major Arcana
Number 33 is the last master number in numerology and is associated with The Lovers in the Major Arcana of the Tarot. The image of The Key seeks to highlight not only the material it is made of but also its lines, revealing whether it is an older or newer key. Symbolically a key suggests undisclosed knowledge and hidden wisdom. Whenever a key is highlighted in a story, it is because it

stores something of inestimable value, some treasure. Thus, The Key also became a reference for those who keep a secret. It may be an unrequited love, or some hidden knowledge to which most people will never have access. In Christianity, for example, the key is associated with St. Peter who holds the keys of Heaven. In other religions and philosophies, a key represents something special that opens and closes.

Minor Arcana

The Eight of Diamonds brings the warning that it is time for you to start important plans in your life. This card represents success where there is commitment and enterprise. At this moment everything that you carry out with dedication and confidence is bound to work. Make your goals come to fruition, do not be afraid to focus on what you believe in and would like to do. Your energy in this period will be conducive for you to focus and do the activities in the most detailed way possible.

Interaction between the Arcana

This card shows the tool needed to promote change in your life. It means that you are closing one cycle and/or starting a new one. To close a cycle, The Key indicates that you should not be afraid to close the door, preventing the past from coming back to bother you. Preventing the past from returning to your home is critical. Only then will the chapter close, and you will be ready for another one to begin. If you have just started a new cycle, this Gypsy card alerts you to the fear of the unknown. It fills the mind with doubts, with memories of failures, with pessimism. All this delays your arrival at the door. Uncertainty then sets in and you are reluctant to use the key and open the door. Do not listen to fear. Give fuel to faith, hope and optimism.

Positive Aspects

It is time for new discoveries and opportunities, The Key will bring you the possibility of success and happiness if you strive for it. The path you need to follow will be very clear, you just need the energy and courage to plunge headlong into the possibilities.

Negative Aspects

Just as doors open with The Key, they can also close. Be very careful not to miss the unique opportunities that will arise in your life for fear of making mistakes. Above all, do not let people you believe are close to you deceive you, causing you to lose your chance to succeed and be happy. It is best to avoid discussing your life plans and goals with those who will not contribute in any way to your achievement.

Work and Finances
This is a phase with lots of positive energy and achievements. Your commitment and dedication to work can earn you a promotion or reward. Stay focused on your career goals and they will bring you visibility and success. If an interesting opportunity appears offering you new challenges, do not be afraid, this will be perfect for your career and your self-esteem. If you are unemployed, that long-awaited interview is likely to come up soon. Best of all, it will open the door to a new phase of your life, be confident that everything will be all right. Have faith and believe in your potential, for you have much good energy within you. Good news will appear soon if you are bold and follow the path that destiny has prepared for you. The Key has appeared to bring you the best opportunities.

Love and Relationship
Single: A door to the path you have been longing for will open, and it seems that there is someone special is on the other side waiting for you. You just need to get out there and go after your dreams, because the world already conspires in your favour.

In a Relationship: Don't be worried about your relationship at this time. What seems like something going wrong will be solved and you will find peace and happiness. Have courage and do everything you dreamed of together. This will strengthen the relationship and bring you closer together.

General Aspects
Opening paths, progress, solutions, realization of an idea, a plan, a positive outflow, help, something or someone who indicates a path. Need for commitment and action, answers, opportunities that bring learning and evolution. End of mysteries, revelation. End of conflicts based on individual decisions and choices. Free will, conscience, courage and determination. It is worth remembering that within esoteric and spiritual philosophies, when we receive or find a key, we are considered initiates. The Key is a symbol that invites us to make a personal effort to overcome difficult situations, those that will bring us inner enlightenment and progress.

Message
It is necessary to know how to use the key that life offers for our own benefit.

Card 34 – The Fish
Element ~ Water

Card number 34 of the Gypsy Deck is known as The Fish. Since ancient times in the Asian culture, it is common to have the representation of the Koi (a type of fish) as a symbol of prosperity and abundance. Its positive expressions do not stop there; in Christianity the figure of the fish is also connected to miracles, faith and good events. In several biblical passages we can see a fish as the symbol of good news.

The Fish in the Gypsy Deck does not change its essence; this card is associated with the Chariot of the Tarot, where achievements and riches are transmitted in their messages. Despite being classified as a neutral card because it depends on all the others that accompany it in a reading, The Fish brings a message of luck and good cycles for investments and gains, especially when we talk about finances. Its concept is based on the great power of multiplication; fish are able to multiply quickly with each cycle of reproduction. As they are a source of sacred food, these animals are considered very special in many cultures and religions.

Major Arcana
The Fish is the card that highlights wealth and prosperity, an aspect closely linked to the meaning of the King of Diamonds. In numerology, The Fish appears in the spirituality chart with number 7 (3+4=7). The image on the card also emphasizes elements that indicate wealth, like coffers or gold coins. The Fish tends to be represented in the shades of gold and orange, reinforcing the interpretation of the card.

Minor Arcana

At this time you don't need to fear difficulties or threats that appear in your way. The King of Diamonds reveals a high level of confidence in your wisdom and ability to analyse situations and your environment. This is a great time to invest in business or enterprising ideas that you may have. The Fish enhances your power to organize affairs and excel in any kind of situation. As a true king would, you will not let yourself down and will stay focused on your goals. This card often depicts a person in whom everyone can put enormous trust, a great counsellor.

Interaction between the Arcana

The appearance of The Fish indicates wealth and luck when we are attentive and prepared to seize the good opportunities that arise in our life. It is related to concrete things - material goods, business and money. This card foretells the possibility of profit in new ventures or that the effort and commitment in our professional activities will be rewarded. The Fish is a symbol of life and abundance, due to its prodigious ability to reproduce with almost infinite amount of roe. The Fish is a strong symbol in China and has also inspired rich iconography among Christian artists; if it carries a ship on its back, it symbolizes Christ and his Church.

Positive Aspects

This will be a time of gain and wealth. The Fish card promises a great stream of good energies that will bring very satisfying accomplishments and many profits whenever great effort is made. This is the perfect time to invest in your dreams. Keep your eyes wide open for any good opportunity that may arise, a door may open briefly for you to achieve success in your life.

Negative Aspects

The obstacles this card can present are associated with the barriers that may come on your way to prevent you from achieving your goals. Keep your focus on what you want and be wise to be able to sidestep these impasses that we are all subject to.

Work and Finances

All the dedication and investment you have put into your career will be recognized. If you own your business, profit and achievements are highly likely. This is the perfect time to take advantage of partnerships that seem to be profitable. If you are unemployed, believe in your potential as The Fish will bring you good energies for success. Despite its indication of neutrality, The Fish corresponds with luck, good opportunities and achievements. Believe in your ability, good harvests are yours for the taking.

Love and Relationship

Single: This card promises good opportunities to meet that special someone. Pay close attention to people who appear in your path, perhaps your great love is just around the corner.

In a Relationship: Expect this to be a stable time if you are in a relationship. A good financial period will leave everything calm for both of you. Fights can often happen because of financial issues, and this good phase will bring a lull so that money worries don't interfere with the good energy of the relationship. Focus on enjoying life with your partner and creating happy memories. This is a great time to plan a holiday together.

General Aspects

Luck, progress, money, life, prosperity, profits, material rewards, financial achievement, abundance, good fortune, wealth, greatness, miracles, multiplication, opulence, accomplishment, concretization of something in the physical plane. It alerts about good energies that will soon take shape in the financial life. The energy of gains and rewards is brought as something important by the Universe. The Fish brings the promise of good fortune, fulfilment of dreams and desires, taking them off the mental plane and bringing them into the physical world. Natural flow of life, flexibility, intuition, and physical/spiritual balance, happiness, contentment, joy, and ascension. Hope for better days to manifest.

Message

Fish live in motion just as we should keep the flow of our lives moving.

Card 35 – The Anchor
Element – Earth

The Anchor is card 35 in the Gypsy Deck. It can bring a positive or a negative message in a reading depending on what is currently happening in your life. The Anchor indicates parking, getting stuck or stopping somewhere. It can bring a negative message if stopping is detrimental to your evolution or development at this time. Be it in a relationship, in the work environment, in relation to finances, it really relates to any or all points that do not get you anywhere or are considered a waste of time. Life is too short to be docked in a port for a long time. The Anchor can also be positive, it can be related to a necessary stop for reflection or organization of life that adds value to commence on a new path, more safely, with a quieter route. The Anchor will not hold you for long, it will not take away your desire to sail the seas of the world to seek and distribute knowledge.

Even if you have already achieved some goals, do not hold back as if your trajectory was limited only to this point. We know that it can be comfortable to settle into what seems safe, but the horizon is far greater than we can see. The possibilities are endless, and not everything that does you well now will last forever. To conquer something and venture onto new paths does not mean that you will need to give up what you have already achieved. You don't always need to discard everything you have to add more dreams and goals to your life.

Major Arcana
The Anchor symbol is related to the sea, and for sailors it is one of the most frequently chosen tattoo designs. It is said that the first sailor who tattooed an

anchor made a great trip crossing the seas and returned safe and sound. Since then seamen see the anchor tattoo as a primordial item and a rite of passage. Nowadays, the anchor tattoo has gained the attention of women because of the symbolic significance, considering that women can be represented by the sea, with their tides and instabilities. The Anchor is a safe harbor, and the certainty that stability will prevail.

Minor Arcana

The Nine of Spades is the most feared card in the pack. It carries a message of a very depressing and lonely energy. It can tell of a period of disgust, enmity and fragility. It can also suggest a phase of conclusions and closures. It is very important, more than ever, to seek strength. Surround yourself with people and things that will do you good. Look for the best way to get through this turbulent time as it will pass.

Interaction between the Arcana

The Anchor tells you to move forward, as far as possible. If necessary, wait for the storm to pass, and then proceed with certainty that you will reach your destiny. We must remember that stability is not synonymous with immobility, and security is not synonymous with a home. The Anchor should not remain longer than the time required on the seabed. We must actively position ourselves before our relationships. If you are experiencing troubled times typical of the Nine of Spades, the Anchor suggests this will bring stability.

Positive Aspects

The positive side of The Anchor suggests a person who spends a lot of time planning for the future; someone who does not enjoy living without goals and perspectives. This is someone, possibly yourself, who needs to analyse the future, choosing which path to take and the possibilities of reaching success as deeply as possible before taking a step.

Negative Aspects

In a negative spread, The Anchor can reflect a very suspicious person. Someone who needs an overwhelming amount of security before considering new goals, so much so that you end up being cocooned in your own nest. With the fear of making mistakes, you might abandon dreams on your journey and miss out on unique experiences. Maybe it's time to pull up The Anchor and go out into the seas, be wise.

Work and Finances
You are someone who seeks stability wherever you are; you need to feel secure in your job and in fact this is your main goal. Dedicate yourself to this ideal, but always look to achieve more knowledge and stand out. This attitude is good for your ego and ensures that if there is a need you will be prepared to face new challenges. If you are unemployed, know that there will be an opportunity coming soon, one in which will feel safe and secure. Allow yourself to evolve, be careful not to stagnate. This card can contain several messages in a reading; to understand it better, it is necessary to reflect upon the context of your life in which it best fits. The most important thing is that you do not lock yourself in one position, allow yourself to seek new directions and horizons.

Love and Relationship
Single: The Anchor represents your sentimental attachment to a past relationship. It's no use looking for someone else when your heart is still full of hopes towards a person from a previous relationship. Sort through your thoughts and feelings first; only then will you be able to find someone who deserves your love.

In a Relationship: If you are in a relationship, this card indicates a lack of affection. You attach yourself to this involvement because it guarantees you stability in some way. Remember that it takes love to build something solid together, so if you want this relationship to continue, evaluate yourself and find the gaps that need to be filled in to make that relationship work.

General Aspects
Security, stability, success, happy life, trust, the foundation of achievements, heritage, reliability, difficulties that are overcome. Happy moments, consolidation, inner certainty, self-confidence, faith and belief in something bringing positive results. Maturity, a need to remain firm in decisions or despair. A positive sign of stability arriving at various levels: mental, spiritual, emotional and physical, because this message always points to something solid and we need to believe. Negatively it can indicate fixed ideas, paralysis and accommodation. In general, this card allows new investments. The Anchor asks you not to give up on your dreams, even the oldest ones, alternatively, it could be time to plan new ideas for the near future.

Message
Safety and stability in life.

Card 36 – The Cross
Element – All

This is the only card that includes metal

Card 36 of the Gypsy Deck is The Cross. Consulters have been known to feel fear when this card appears in a reading. This is because of the Christian symbolism that refers to anguish, pain and ordeal. We must pay attention to the real meaning of The Cross in this deck. This card does relate to the passage of Christ, but its meaning is much deeper and is part of the spiritual essence. It reflects the most beautiful faith and strength over all that afflicts us and desires us evil. Jesus carried the Cross to prove that he believed in the divine promises, and this is how you should feel: a person filled with spiritual power that is blessed. The future awaits you with open arms to bring the rewards you deserve.

The cross also has meaning in other philosophies. There is a popular saying: "We all have a cross to bear!" Be proud of yours, it is nothing more than proof of how strong and true you are to your principles. In the Gypsy Deck, the Cross is a symbol of victory and wealth of spirit, it carries a good energy of achievements. When The Cross appears in a reading, it brings a message of joys and rewards for who you are and for everything you have done so far.

Major Arcana
The symbol of the Cross arose long before Christianity. Its sides were originally of equal size, with the intersection being right in the middle of the lines, much like the symbol of + (plus). And that version, known as the Greek Cross, although found in diverse locations around the world, had a clear definition. At that time the Cross was a symbol used to represent, among other things, the

union of heaven and earth, the union of opposites, and expansion equally towards all directions. Even today The Cross is used with this particular meaning. There are more than 20 different types of symbols that can represent a cross, still in use today with the most varied meanings. The Cross of The Gypsy Deck maintains the meaning of the union of opposites and balance. It brings a message of the glory of victory and foretells that your goals will be achieved. To achieve success, effort will be required on your part.

Minor Arcana

The Six of Clubs gloriously symbolizes success in everything in life, but its main message is the warning that you need to be a controlled and a humble person, thoughtful and always careful not to speak without thinking. You can enjoy good times in life, The Six of Clubs brings you a message of accomplishments. The strongest message from this card is the warning that if your vanity is exalted, your ego will be able to dominate you and such attitudes can bring you down.

Interaction between the Arcana

Representing the last card of The Gypsy Deck, The Cross has a special meaning. Do not be deceived that it only relates to something that is painful or demands painful sacrifices without rewards in this lifetime. This idea is tied to the cross used as a Christian symbol of the martyrdom suffered by Christ. Contrasting with the Six of Clubs, it means entrepreneurship and action. The Cross also represents the union of the spiritual with the material. In this sense, it reveals a balanced person, who can travel between the two worlds and manages to feed well both his spiritual and material needs. A person protected by the Divine and Karmic laws.

Positive Aspects

Believe in everything you have chosen and done until this moment in your life. What should be sown is in its proper place now and soon you will find the peace you seek, the love that you dream of and most importantly, much knowledge and evolution, both mental and spiritual. Good news will soon come your way and you can benefit from all the deserved happiness. Even if barriers arise, you have the strength to overcome them, never get discouraged.

Negative Aspects

The negative side of this card expresses an alert to not allow your lack of faith to push you further down when trials appear; beware of bad thoughts. Another important warning is about betrayal of someone close to you, be careful who you currently trust.

Work and Finances
Beware of emotional and physical wear. There may be a lot of unnecessary gossip going on. You may be afraid and fearful at present. The Cross tells you to be confident and act with conviction. Good times are on the way, you will be valued and recognized. It is important that you don't give up. For those who are unemployed and looking for something, know that The Cross of The Gypsy Deck asks you to continue to search for what you believe. Its value is evident and soon the right opportunity will arise, believe in it and always value yourself. There is nothing to fear if you don't lose faith. The Cross reminds us of the true purpose of our struggles and longings, showing that we can achieve what we want and live our most beautiful dreams, we only need to believe.

Love and Relationship
Single: The Cross represents a new love which will come full of deep and true feelings, it is highly likely to be something lasting and very serious.

In a Relationship: The Cross in love portrays the arrival of a good time for couples. It nullifies the possibility of separation if you have been disagreeing with your partner. The best way forward is communication, make it your main ally and soon everything will be in complete peace and surrender.

General Aspects
Victory, destiny, ascension, positivity, faith, self-confidence, spiritual wisdom, supremacy, improvements, favours, goals successfully achieved. Success and salvation which ends a difficult period of suffering and uncertainty. The triumph, life fills us with maturity. The solution, destiny and inner treasure must be found by each one of us. **It is the best card in the Gypsy Deck** and reminds you to never give up on your ideals. A key of the heavens which can transform pains and sacrifices into protection, liberation and victory.

Message
Happiness and salvation, things will be solved.

Card Combinations

To read with this deck accurately, a study of each of the cards and their possible combinations is required. Whenever you can, open the deck, choose two cards randomly and identify how they interact with each other. Start by selecting two cards; later when you feel more confident work with three cards and then five.

Next, write a random question about a fictitious person and open the deck trying to identify the answer to that subject. By focusing on a specific subject you will better understand how each card has an answer to each type of question, be it emotional, physical or spiritual.

These combinations are essentially a guide. Over time, the more familiarity you have with the cards the greater your confidence will be, and your intuition will become stronger.

The cards are listed twice because it matters which card appears first. For example, if The Ring appears first in front of The Coffin, it announces separation. If The Coffin appears first and The Ring after, it means the end of a relationship and the beginning of a new one.

Card 1 - The Rider

Rider + Clover	Small problems coming.
Clover + Rider	Overcoming problems, quick fixes.
Rider + Ship	Changes coming.
Ship + Rider	Internal changes are required.
Rider + House	Person who arrives in your life.
House + Rider	Person who leaves your life.
Rider + Tree	Act quickly to achieve security.
Tree + Rider	Realization of projects in a safe way.
Rider + Cloud	Passing moments of difficulty.
Cloud + Reader	Situation clearing quickly.
Rider + Snake	Person interested only in sex.
Snake + Rider	Discovering betrayal.
Rider + Coffin	Transformation.
Coffin + Rider	Changes bringing news.
Rider + Bouquet	Realization of dreams, arrival of new love.
Bouquet + Rider	Balance coming into a situation.
Rider + Sickle	Appropriate ending (cut) coming into a situation.
Sickle + Rider	News about plans and/or projects.
Rider + Whip	Situation that repeats itself.
Whip + Rider	Situation or person that comes back from the past.
Rider + Birds	Situation developing positively.
Birds + Rider	Good changes with greater communication.
Rider + Child	Good news bringing joy and new beginnings.
Child + Rider	Immature in the way of acting and thinking.
Rider + Fox	Act with cunning, think of strategies to achieve goals.
Fox + Rider	Trap that will require speediness for an effective solution.
Rider + Bear	Beware of false and jealous people.
Bear + Rider	End of a domineering situation.
Rider + Star	Dreams coming true with spiritual help
Star + Rider	Trust your own intuition to open your ways.
Rider + Stork	Unexpected pregnancy.
Stork + Rider	Look for new ways to improve a situation.
Rider + Dog	Arrival of loyal friends - change of life.
Dog + Rider	Lean on friends and their loyalty.

Rider + Tower	End of period of solitude and depression.
Tower + Rider	Isolate for internal reassessment and personal evolution.
Rider + Garden	Period of peace, tranquillity and stability arriving.
Garden + Rider	Socialize.
Rider + Mountain	Complicated phase coming. Do not run away, face it.
Mountain + Rider	Quick overcoming of energy consuming problems.
Rider + Path	More than one path to choose in a situation.
Path + Rider	The choice was made the right way, wait for good news.
Rider + Rat	Beware of a person/situation consuming your energy.
Rat + Rider	A stressful situation will change quickly, bringing news.
Rider + Heart	Emotional news coming, bringing joy and security.
Heart + Rider	New love, new feelings, new emotional paths.
Rider + Ring	Good period coming from alliances in every way, enjoy.
Ring + Rider	Alliances that were formed bringing a new phase of joy and stability.
Rider + Book	Seize the opportunities that will arise from new work and study.
Book + Rider	Keep details of plans, projects, work and studies to yourself.
Rider + Letter	Wait for news that will quickly move your life.
Letter + Rider	Take all you know, news you have received and give direction to your life.
Rider + Gypsy Man	Dynamic man, agile, courageous, full of ideas and attitudes.
Gypsy Man + Rider	Always a man close to you, possibly a relative.
Rider + Gypsy Woman	Determined, independent woman in control of her life.
Gypsy Woman + Rider	A woman who is always present, possibly a relative.
Rider + Lily	A period of peace, tranquillity and growth in the emotional area.
Lily + Rider	Use wisdom and a little coldness to deal with the phase that will come.
Rider + Sun	A new phase of realizations, projects fulfilled, dreams realized.
Sun + Rider	Do not run away from reality, do not hide.
Rider + Moon	Look within yourself for answers and intuitive paths.
Moon + Rider	Intuition quickly bringing new directions into a situation.
Rider + Key	Seek new solutions to life.

Key + Rider	No more surprises, enjoy the new options in life.
Rider + Fish	Seek material progress, go after financial goals.
Fish + Rider	Money arriving. Prosperity coming quickly.
Rider + Anchor	New things will not come if there is no movement.
Anchor + Rider	The security you are looking for will arrive quickly.
Rider + Cross	Seek to overcome difficulties and pains.
Cross + Rider	All that had to be surpassed has been. Now the happy ending arrives.

Card 2 - The Clover

Clover + Rider	Overcoming problems, quick fixes.
Rider + Clover	Small problems coming.
Clover + Ship	Problems on a journey.
Ship + Clover	Stay away from problems.
Clover + House	Family problems.
House + Clover	House, property with problems.
Clover + Tree	Problems removing stability and security.
Tree + Clover	Look for your roots to ward off problems.
Clover + Cloud	Difficulties are causing mental confusion.
Cloud + Clover	Lack of clear-thinking bringing problems.
Clover + Snake	Complicated attitudes bringing betrayal.
Snake + Clover	Situation of treacherous opportunism.
Clover + Coffin	Problems causing negative transformation in the situation.
Coffin + Clover	Negative and problematic changes.
Clover + Bouquet	Problems being overcome with balance.
Bouquet + Clover	Lack of emotional balance.
Clover + Sickle	Problems being cut out.
Sickle + Clover	Attitudes bringing problems to the surface.
Clover + Whip	Problems are likely to persist for a while.
Whip + Clover	Insisting on the same attitude is the cause for so many problems, change.
Clover + Birds	The difficulties and small problems will be temporary.
Birds + Clover	Increase communication to overcome your problem
Clover + Child	Ingenuity causing problems.
Child + Clover	Problems with children, grandchildren, nephews or nieces.
Clover + Fox	Problems and pitfalls in the situation.
Fox + Clover	Use cleverness to overcome problems.
Clover + Bear	Problems with organization and administration of the situation.
Bear + Clover	Protect yourself in the situation to solve problems.
Clover + Star	Spiritual problems.
Star + Clover	Overcoming problems with divine help.
Clover + Stork	Problems causing you to change course.

Stork + Clover	New situation bringing problems.
Clover + Dog	Troubled relationship with friends.
Dog + Clover	Friends/friendship going through problems.
Clover + Tower	Spiritual problems and distancing.
Tower + Clover	Difficulty at personal, intimate level.
Clover + Garden	Several small problems in having social relationships.
Garden + Clover	Social relationships with problems.
Clover + Mountain	Problems of all kinds.
Mountain + Clover	Big and small problems.
Clover + Path	Difficulties making choices.
Path + Clover	Paths full of problems.
Clover + Rat	Stressful, mental problems.
Rat + Clover	Mental stress bringing problems.
Clover + Heart	Emotional problems.
Heart + Clover	Feelings causing problems.
Clover + Ring	Relationship problems.
Ring + Clover	**This combination will bring trouble.**
Clover + Book	Educational and professional problems.
Book + Clover	Troubled secrets.
Clover + Letter	Difficulties with documents. Difficulty in communicating.
Letter + Clover	News of problems.
Clover + Gypsy Man	Difficulties with a man.
Gypsy Man + Clover	**Man bringing trouble.**
Clover + Gypsy Woman	Difficulties with a woman.
Gypsy Woman + Clover	**Woman bringing trouble.**
Clover + Lily	Problems in having peace and happiness.
Lily + Clover	Emotional coldness bringing trouble.
Clover + Sun	Problems that cannot be hidden.
Sun + Clover	Clear solution to the difficulties.
Clover + Moon	Difficulty in connecting to the spiritual.
Moon + Clover	Intuition showing the problems.
Clover + Key	Problems in finding solutions in a situation.
Key + Clover	Solving problems.
Clover + Fish	Financial problems.
Fish + Clover	The material world bringing problems.
Clover + Anchor	Security issues.

Anchor + Clover		Attachment to problems.
Clover + Cross		Proof of faith.
Cross + Clover		End of problems.

Card 3 - The Ship

Ship + Rider   Requiring internal changes.
Rider + Ship   Changes coming.
Ship + Clover   Stay away from problems.
Clover + Ship   Problems on a journey.
Ship + Home   Return home.
House + Ship   Change of residence.
Ship + Tree   Unstable health.
Tree + Ship   Stable situation coming.
Ship + Cloud   Travel that has not yet been decided.
Cloud + Ship   Journey provoked by mental confusion.
Ship + Snake   **Instability provoked by betrayal.**
Snake + Ship   Betrayal causing change of course.
Ship + Coffin   Cancellation of travel.
Coffin + Ship   Long-term change of plans.
Ship + Bouquet   Balanced, stable and happy journey.
Bouquet + Ship   Good walks, journey of balance and happiness.
Ship + Sickle   Travel bringing cuts and course changes.
Sickle + Ship   Cancellation of a planned trip. Change of plans.
Ship + Whip   Travel with suffering. Painful journey.
Whip + Ship   **Pursue the journey despite obstacles.**
Ship + Birds   Successful travel with group of people.
Birds + Ship   Communicate on travels.
Ship + Child   Trip to new places.
Child + Ship   Tours with children.
Ship + Fox   Well planned trip.
Fox + Ship   Traps coming, be careful.
Ship + Bear   Displacements required for self-protection.
Bear + Ship   Search for distant safety.
Ship + Star   Travel and displacement of success.
Star + Ship   Astral travel. Dreams.
Ship + Stork   Journey to good news.
Stork + Ship   Air travel.
Ship + Dog   Travel with friends.
Dog + Ship   Distant friend.
Ship + Tower   Solitary journey.

Tower + Ship	Journey into yourself.
Ship + Garden	Long journey.
Garden + Ship	Party, socialization outside the comfort zone.
Ship + Mountain	Journey with difficulties.
Mountain + Ship	Problems changing slowly.
Ship + Path	Travel by land.
Path + Ship	More than one option of places to choose from.
Ship + Rat	Confusing journey causing stress.
Rat + Ship	Wait for the right time to travel or move.
Ship + Heart	Emotional, sentimental journey.
Heart + Ship	Distant feelings, feelings ending.
Ship + Ring	Travel with a partner.
Ring + Ship	Travel after formalized alliance.
Ship + Book	Professional or study related travel.
Book + Ship	New job, position, professional opportunity coming.
Ship + Letter	Departure in search of information, documents. Changes in solutions.
Letter + Ship	Invitations to travel.
Ship + Gypsy Man	Displacement for or with a man.
Gypsy Man + Ship	A distant man, coming slowly.
Ship + Gypsy Woman	Displacement for or with a woman.
Gypsy Woman + Ship	A distant woman coming slowly.
Ship + Lily	Long-distance travel
Lily + Ship	Change of place causing coldness in the situation.
Ship + Sun	Travel overseas.
Sun + Ship	New horizons, success.
Ship + Moon	Romantic journey.
Moon + Ship	Travel by own merit.
Ship + Letter	Solutions changes.
Key + Ship	Solving problems to move around.
Ship + Fish	Travel or change of place bringing prosperity.
Fish + Ship	Expensive trip.
Ship + Anchor	Travel stopped, boring.
Anchor + Ship	Security providing travel.
Ship + Cross	Journey of faith, in search of faith.
Cross + Ship	End of situation bringing slow changes.

Card 4 - The House

House + Rider	Independent person.
Rider + House	Person who arrives in your life.
House + Clover	House or property with problems.
Clover + House	Family problems.
House + Ship	Change of residence.
Ship + Home	Return home.
House + Tree	Home strengthened.
Tree + House	Family growth.
House + Cloud	Time of confusion at home.
Cloud + House	Family imbalance.
House + Snake	Seek internal balance to deal with betrayal.
Snake + House	Family betrayal, marital.
House + Coffin	The family going through a phase of great change.
Coffin + House	Marital separation.
House + Bouquet	Balanced family.
Bouquet + House	Happiness in the home.
House + Sickle	**Family separation.**
Sickle + House	Sale of house, property.
House + Whip	Family violence.
Whip + House	Another family, another family situation.
House + Birds	Romance between the couple.
Birds + House	Gossip in the family.
House + Child	Family in a new phase, possible birth, pregnancy.
Child + House	Children, grandchildren, nephews or nieces.
House + Fox	Theft in the family, in the house.
Fox + House	Use cunning to acquire real estate.
House + Bear	Protected family, who protect each other.
Bear + House	Investment in real estate.
House + Star	Spiritual family. Ancestors.
Star + House	Family achievement.
House + Stork	Renovation of property. Internal changes.
Stork + House	New house, change of residence.
House + Dog	A united and loyal family.
Dog + House	Neighbours, people nearby.
House + Tower	Spiritual balance.

Tower + House	Look within. Energy rebalancing.
House + Garden	Large and/or dispersed family.
Garden + House	Keep a certain distance from the family.
House + Mountain	Family in trouble.
Mountain + House	Problems being brought home.
House + Path	Distant property, new location.
Path + House	Search for new family ways.
House + Rat	Family relationship worn.
Rat + House	Stress affecting the family.
Home + Heart	Emotional balance.
Heart + House	Loving and emotional family.
House + Ring	Marriage, stable situation, family constitution.
Ring + Home	Buy, sell or rent property.
House + Book	Family business and work with relative.
Book + Home	Home office, work from home.
House + Letter	Family documents, inventory, deed.
Letter + Home	News for the family.
House + Gypsy Man	Balanced man, structured.
Gypsy Man + House	Father, grandfather, uncle, master of the house.
House + Gypsy Woman	Balanced, structured woman.
Gypsy Woman + House	Mother, grandmother, aunt, mistress of the house.
House + Lily	Old house/property. Property of family heirloom.
Lily + House	Find more wisdom in family relationships.
House + Sun	Family in the phase of happiness.
Sun + House	Clarity in the family relationship.
House + Moon	Property or house of dreams.
Moon + House	Deserved property.
Home + Key	Family helping with solutions.
Key + House	New house.
House + Fish	Prosperous family, large family.
Fish + House	Family financial growth coming up.
House + Anchor	Stable family.
Anchor + House	Trapped in a family situation.
House + Cross	Church, religious space.
Cross + House	Family victory.

Card 5 - The Tree

Tree + Rider	Realization of projects in a safe way.
Rider + Tree	Act quickly to achieve security.
Tree + Clover	Look for your roots to ward off problems.
Clover + Tree	Problems removing stability and security.
Tree + Ship	Stable situation coming.
Ship + Tree	Unstable health.
Tree + House	Family growth.
House + Tree	Home strengthened.
Tree + Cloud	Hidden disease, difficult to diagnose.
Cloud + Tree	Mental illness, mental confusion.
Tree + Cobra	Health/disease of the genital and reproductive organs.
Snake + Tree	Ancient betrayal, obsessed lover.
Tree + Coffin	Serious illness, there may be no cure.
Coffin + Tree	Complete change of life.
Tree + Bouquet	Good health.
Bouquet + Tree	Balance and happiness strengthening security.
Tree + Sickle	Surgery, invasive procedure.
Sickle + Tree	**Health issues, physical security, growth.**
Tree + Whip	Long lasting disease, recurrent disease.
Whip + Tree	Physical pain, heavy exercise.
Tree + Birds	Security and growth in communications.
Birds + Tree	Nature. Building conversations.
Tree + Child	Good change in health. Finding a cure.
Child + Tree	New phase of stability.
Tree + Fox	Hidden disease. Physical traps.
Fox + Tree	Wrongly diagnosed disease. Seek a second opinion
Tree + Bear	Obesity, food disturbance.
Bear + Tree	Manage the situation more safely.
Tree + Star	Spiritual treatment.
Star + Tree	Physical healing.
Tree + Stork	Physical recovery.
Stork + Tree	Go for growth and stability.
Tree + Dog	Medical team, health professionals.
Dog + Tree	Twin soul, strong and true friendship.
Tree + Tower	Interior growth.

Tower + Tree	Individual plans.
Tree + Garden	Linked to nature, to seek nature.
Garden + Tree	Social security.
Tree + Mountain	Serious health problems.
Mountain + Tree	Fatigue and insecurity.
Tree + Path	Branching path options.
Path + Tree	Change of life in search of security.
Tree + Rat	**Nervousness and stress taking root.**
Rat + Tree	General health problems. Check-up needed.
Tree + Heart	Magnification of feelings. Heart problems.
Heart + Tree	Emotional creation of roots.
Tree + Ring	Relationship stable and secure. Long-term agreement.
Ring + Tree	A new alliance bringing stability.
Tree + Book	Disease that has not yet been detected.
Book + Tree	Keep plans for growth a secret.
Tree + Letter	Medical examination, the result of health examinations.
Letter + Tree	News of growth and stability.
Tree + Gypsy Man	Sick man. Physical, emotional and spiritual diseases
Gypsy Man + Tree	Man who heals, doctor, connected to medical area.
Tree + Gypsy Woman	Sick woman. Physical, emotional and spiritual diseases.
Gypsy Woman + Tree	Woman who heals, doctor, connected to medical area.
Tree + Lily	Sexual health, sexual disease.
Lily + Tree	Wisdom and a certain coldness bringing growth.
Tree + Sun	Situation of strength and happiness.
Sun + Tree	Physical, emotional and spiritual healing.
Tree + Moon	Spiritual security.
Moon + Tree	Secret meeting, something hidden.
Tree + Key	Growth by expanding solutions.
Key + Tree	Seek new ways of growth.
Tree + Fish	Seek stability to have prosperity.
Fish + Tree	Cash input bringing growth.
Tree + Anchor	Safe growth. Stable health.
Anchor + Tree	Safety that brings growth.
Tree + Cross	Person, situation of great faith. Frequent physical pain.
Cross + Tree	Completion bringing security.

Card 6 - The Clouds

Cloud + Rider	Situation clearing quickly.
Rider + Cloud	Passing moments of difficulty.
Cloud + Clover	Lack of clear thinking bringing problems.
Clover + Cloud	Difficulties are causing mental confusion.
Cloud + Ship	Journey provoked by mental confusion.
Ship + Cloud	Travel that has not yet been decided.
Cloud + House	Family imbalance.
House + Cloud	Home going through a time of confusion.
Cloud + Tree	Mental illness, mental confusion.
Tree + Cloud	Hidden disease, difficult to diagnose.
Cloud + Snake	Hidden, undiscovered betrayal.
Snake + Cloud	Homosexuality.
Cloud + Coffin	Clarity, change of thoughts.
Coffin + Cloud	Confusing change, no immediate solutions.
Cloud + Bouquet	Confused, looking for clearer thinking.
Bouquet+ Cloud	Balance of thoughts shaken.
Cloud + Sickle	Irrational decision.
Sickle + Cloud	Problems with recurrent thoughts.
Cloud + Whip	Thoughts that cause pain and suffering.
Whip + Cloud	Old sadness bringing mental confusion.
Cloud + Birds	Lying gossip.
Birds + Cloud	Complicated conversations.
Cloud + Child	Concern with children, grandchildren, nephews or nieces.
Child + Cloud	Child with attention deficit.
Cloud + Fox	Doubtful character.
Fox + Cloud	Mental traps.
Cloud + Bear	Fear and insecurity.
Bear + Cloud	Mental domination causing confusion.
Cloud + Star	Act, do not procrastinate.
Star + Cloud	A situation of mental confusion that quickly dissipates.
Cloud + Stork	Wrong bet, wrong choice.
Stork + Cloud	Search to discover, to find, to clear.
Cloud + Dog	Judgment wrong, not clear.
Dog + Cloud	Unreliable friend.

Cloud + Tower	Depression, mental or psychological confusion.
Tower + Cloud	Spiritual possessors.
Cloud + Garden	Uncertainty in projects.
Garden + Cloud	Magnification of confused thoughts.
Cloud + Mountain	Confused thoughts about problems.
Mountain + Cloud	Indecision with a problematic situation.
Cloud + Path	Great mental confusion.
Path + Cloud	Indecision, confusing paths, unclear options.
Cloud + Rat	Mental confusion that corrodes, destroys, stresses.
Rat + Cloud	Stress causing worries and sorrows.
Cloud + Heart	Indecision in love.
Heart + Cloud	Conflicting feelings.
Cloud + Ring	Relationship problems, lack of clarity and common vision.
Ring + Cloud	Problematic alliance, uncertain contracts.
Cloud + Book	Secrets that bring sorrow and confusion.
Book + Cloud	Confusing professional period.
Cloud + Letter	Difficulty of communication.
Letter + Cloud	Confusing news, lacking in truth.
Cloud + Gypsy Man	Man who hides his true self, fake.
Gypsy Man + Cloud	Unstable, confused, indecisive man.
Cloud + Gypsy Woman	Woman who hides her true self, fake.
Gypsy Woman + Cloud	Unstable, confused, indecisive woman.
Cloud + Lily	Unrest, loss of peace.
Lily + Cloud	Lack of wisdom in a situation.
Cloud + Sun	Lack of clarity, thoughts and vision.
Sun + Cloud	Accept what cannot be changed.
Cloud + Moon	Uncertainty of thoughts.
Moon + Cloud	Achievements without merit.
Cloud + Key	Confused thoughts do not allow finding solutions.
Key + Cloud	Solutions to clarify thoughts. Therapy.
Cloud + Fish	Materialistic thinking. Hidden money.
Fish + Cloud	Financial uncertainties, unfavourable financial matters.
Cloud + Anchor	Thoughts affecting safety.
Anchor + Cloud	Great mental instability.
Cloud + Cross	Lack of faith, spiritual doubts.
Cross + Cloud	Uncertain victory.

Card 7 - The Snake

Snake + Rider	Betrayal being discovered.
Rider + Snake	Person interested only in sex.
Snake + Clover	Situation of treacherous opportunism.
Clover + Snake	Complicated attitudes bringing betrayal.
Snake + Ship	Betrayal causing change of course.
Ship + Snake	Instability provoked by betrayal.
Snake + House	Family betrayal, marital unfaithfulness.
House + Snake	Seek internal balance to deal with betrayal.
Snake + Tree	Ancient betrayal, obsessed lover.
Tree + Snake	Health/disease of the genital or reproductive organs.
Snake + Cloud	Homosexuality.
Cloud + Snake	Hidden, undiscovered betrayal.
Snake + Coffin	Fast changes, losing the game.
Coffin + Snake	A situation that changes due to betrayal.
Snake + Bouquet	Affectionate and kind sex.
Bouquet + Snake	Lack of balance caused by betrayal.
Snake + Sickle	Betrayal provoking pain and endings.
Sickle + Snake	Lack of libido, impotence.
Snake + Whip	Promiscuity, rough sex.
Whip + Snake	Repeated betrayal, injuries, sexual abuse.
Snake + Birds	Group sex, sex at the heart of the matter.
Birds + Snake	Slander, lies.
Snake + Child	A malicious person who uses naive people.
Child + Snake	Agitated child, Attention Deficit Syndrome.
Snake + Fox	Great betrayal. Breach of promise.
Fox + Snake	Traps that led to betrayal.
Snake + Bear	Betrayal of feelings, of affection.
Bear + Snake	A person who likes morbid sex.
Snake + Star	Feeling of spiritual betrayal, of unworthiness.
Star + Snake	Quick, agile resolution taken.
Snake + Stork	Route deviation.
Stork + Snake	Difficult change about to happen.
Snake + Dog	Betrayal of a trust.
Dog + Snake	Unfaithful, false friend.
Snake + Tower	Negative thoughts of betrayal.

Tower + Snake	Negative spirit, something false.
Snake + Garden	A person who stands out in physical appearance.
Garden + Snake	Lack of social interaction.
Snake + Mountain	Powerful foe promoting betrayals.
Mountain + Snake	**Problems caused by betrayal.**
Snake + Path	Escape, person who hides, someone who doesn't walk.
Path + Snake	Path with many twists and turns, dubious ways.
Snake + Rat	Great worsening of confusion.
Rat + Snake	Anxiety, lost person, suffering.
Snake + Heart	Hate.
Heart + Cobra	Feeling of revenge.
Snake + Ring	Marital betrayal.
Ring + Snake	Intense relationship.
Snake + Book	Secret lover. Hidden sexual desire.
Book + Snake	Unpleasant secret. Professional betrayal.
Snake + Letter	Betrayal coming out, being discovered.
Letter + Snake	Unpleasant News.
Snake + Gypsy Man	Betrayal by a Man.
Gypsy Man + Snake	Seductive, sensual man who likes sex.
Snake + Gypsy Woman	Betrayal by a woman.
Gypsy Woman + Snake	Seductive, sensual woman who likes sex.
Snake + Lily	Sexual desire, sexual attraction.
Lily + Snake	Intense sexual relationship.
Snake + Sun	Agility bringing success. Resolution of a situation.
Sun + Snake	Face a difficult situation.
Snake + Moon	Deception, loss of what was guaranteed.
Moon + Snake	**Results achieved through betrayal.**
Snake + Key	Acting fast to get the solutions.
Key + Snake	**Discovery of betrayal.**
Snake + Fish	**Betrayal for money.**
Fish + Snake	Material and financial problems.
Snake + Anchor	**Betrayal and insecurity.**
Anchor + Snake	Stable relationship with lover.
Snake + Cross	Difficult and dangerous journey.
Cross + Snake	Faith being put to the test.

Card 8 - The Coffin

Coffin + Rider	Changes made bringing news.
Rider + Coffin	Transformation
Coffin + Clover	Negative and problematic changes.
Clover + Coffin	Problems causing negative transformation in the situation.
Coffin + Ship	Long-term change of plans.
Ship + Coffin	Cancellation of travel.
Coffin + House	Marital separation.
House + Coffin	Family going through a phase of great change.
Coffin + Tree	Complete change of life.
Tree + Coffin	Serious illness, there may be no cure.
Coffin + Cloud	Confused change, no immediate solutions.
Cloud + Coffin	Clarity, change of thoughts.
Coffin + Snake	A situation that changes due to betrayal.
Snake + Coffin	**Fast changes and unlucky gambling.**
Coffin + Bouquet	Positive and sincere transformation.
Bouquet + Coffin	Happiness going away, ending.
Coffin + Sickle	Changes making deep cuts in a situation.
Sickle + Coffin	Severe and recurrent disease.
Coffin + Whip	Pain, painful changes that happen again.
Whip + Coffin	Physical attack, violence.
Coffin + Birds	**Change of subject, actions that differ from words.**
Birds + Coffin	Sad things that bring change.
Coffin + Child	Possible abortion.
Child + Coffin	End of innocence, of irresponsibility.
Coffin + Fox	End of lies, of cleverness. Traps that fail.
Fox + Coffin	Use cunning and cleverness to achieve change.
Coffin + Bear	Losses and annoyances. Person passed away.
Bear + Coffin	Lack of vital energy, lack of passion for life, person without strength.
Coffin + Star	Positive transformation.
Star + Coffin	Intuition helping in times of transition.
Coffin + Stork	Change the way you act, want and think.
Stork + Coffin	Boredom, monotony, lack of goals.
Coffin + Dog	Start of a friendship.

Dog + Coffin	Friend who needs help.
Coffin + Tower	Possible death or risk of dying.
Tower + Coffin	End of solitude.
Coffin + Garden	Social event cancellation. End of a social relationship.
Garden + Coffin	Changes brought about by external events. Lack of control.
Coffin + Mountain	Unfair, problematic change of circumstances.
Mountain + Coffin	Definitive solution of a problem.
Coffin + Path	More than one way to change, choice of change to make.
Path + Coffin	End of the road, paths closed, there are no options.
Coffin + Rat	Change of stressful situation.
Rat + Coffin	Big losses.
Coffin + Heart	End of feelings, dislike of something or someone.
Heart + Coffin	Feelings and emotions calling for radical changes.
Coffin + Ring	Separation, divorce.
Ring + Coffin	Transformative alliance.
Coffin + Book	Change of area of work, profession, studies.
Book + Coffin	Knowledge bringing about a radical change. Secret revealed.
Coffin + Letter	Radical change in the way you communicate.
Letter + Coffin	Lost message, lack of communication.
Coffin + Gypsy Man	Changes and transformations for or in a man.
Gypsy Man + Coffin	Sick, depressed, dissatisfied man; a cheater.
Coffin + Gypsy Woman	Changes and transformations for or in a woman.
Gypsy Woman + Coffin	Sick, depressed, dissatisfied woman; a cheater.
Coffin + Lily	Loss of tranquillity. Rupture, separation.
Lily + Coffin	Tranquillity bringing a great turnaround.
Coffin + Sun	Loss of energy, discouragement.
Sun + Coffin	Total renovation.
Coffin + Moon	Loss of creativity, mental illness.
Moon + Coffin	Dreams and plans being made.
Coffin + Key	Positive changes, solutions.
Key + Coffin	Seek solutions, act to change.
Coffin + Fish	Could be a funeral, change of life.
Fish + Coffin	Financial loss, change of status.
Coffin + Anchor	Loss of stability.
Anchor + Coffin	Transformations are stuck and do not happen.

Coffin + Cross   Changes with victories.
Cross + Coffin   Aggravation of disease, worsening of health.

Card 9 - The Bouquet

Bouquet + Rider	Balance coming into the situation.
Rider + Bouquet	Realization of dreams, arrival of new love.
Bouquet + Clover	Lack of emotional balance.
Clover + Bouquet	Problems being overcome with balance.
Bouquet+ Ship	Good walks, journey of balance and happiness.
Ship + Bouquet	Balanced, stable and happy journey.
Bouquet + House	Happiness in the home.
House + Bouquet	Balanced family.
Bouquet + Tree	Balance and happiness strengthening security.
Tree + Bouquet	Good health.
Bouquet + Cloud	Balance of shaken thoughts.
Cloud + Bouquet	Confusion, search for clearer thinking.
Bouquet + Snake	Lack of balance caused by betrayal.
Snake + Bouquet	Affectionate sex.
Bouquet + Coffin	Happiness going away, ending.
Coffin + Bouquet	Positive and sincere transformation.
Bouquet + Sickle	Positive decisions. Surgery successful.
Sickle + Bouquet	Loss of happiness, balance and success.
Bouquet + Whip	Night-time fun, hectic party.
Whip + Bouquet	Precarious balance.
Bouquet + Birds	Invitation for meeting with known people.
Birds + Bouquet	Animated conversation.
Bouquet + Child	Pure, innocent happiness.
Child + Bouquet	Happy child. Emotional balance.
Bouquet + Fox	Success at risk.
Fox + Bouquet	Emotional trap.
Bouquet + Bear	Support bringing safety.
Bear + Bouquet	Balance being destroyed. Instability, feeling of pressure.
Bouquet + Star	Perfect gift.
Star+ Bouquet	Hope, dreams come true.
Bouquet + Stork	Unexpected pregnancy. Adoption.
Stork + Bouquet	Positive change, happy.
Bouquet + Dog	Gain something that awaits.
Dog + Bouquet	Complete, loyal, balanced friendship.

Bouquet + Tower	Be well with yourself, get out of solitude, be able to exteriorize your joy.
Tower + Ship	Balanced spirituality.
Ship + Garden	Great balance, happiness.
Garden + Bouquet	Successful social event.
Bouquet + Mountain	Happiness that takes time to happen. Difficult balance.
Mountain + Bouquet	Difficulties and emotional problems. Imbalance, instability.
Bouquet + Path	Good opportunities in all areas.
Path + Bouquet	Correct choice of course of life.
Bouquet + Rat	Unpleasant surprises.
Rat + Bouquet	Lack of balance, unhappiness.
Bouquet + Heart	Happiness in love.
Heart + Ship	Feelings of happiness, balance, success.
Ship + Ring	Soul mate, happiness and union.
Ring + Bouquet	Happy marriage, union with happiness.
Bouquet + Book	Professional balance.
Book + Bouquet	Successful studies, great learning.
Bouquet + Letter	Positive solution related to documents, paperwork.
Letter + Bouquet	Invitation or surprising news with a happy result.
Bouquet + Gypsy Man	Happiness, success, balance from a man.
Gypsy Man + Bouquet	Handsome, happy and attractive man.
Bouquet + Gypsy Woman	Happiness, success, balance to or from a woman.
Gypsy Woman + Bouquet	Beautiful, happy and attractive woman.
Bouquet + Lily	Harmony and contentment. Peace.
Lily + Bouquet	Expanded happiness.
Bouquet + Sun	Celebration of great success.
Sun + Bouquet	Perfection.
Bouquet + Moon	Keep feelings more guarded, hidden.
Moon + Bouquet	Deserved satisfaction and success.
Bouquet + Key	Discovering the path of happiness.
Key + Bouquet	Perfect solution, indisputable.
Bouquet + Fish	Gift of value, something expensive, costly.
Fish + Bouquet	Financial situation bringing balance and success.
Bouquet + Anchor	Enduring happiness that does not end.
Anchor + Bouquet	Goals achieved.
Bouquet + Cross	To give, to do something for someone else, charity.

Cross + Bouquet   Happy destiny.

Card 10 - The Sickle

Sickle + Rider	News about plans and/or projects.
Rider + Sickle	Right decision coming into a situation.
Sickle + Clover	Attitudes creating more problems.
Clover + Sickle	Problems being resolved.
Sickle + Ship	Cancellation of a planned trip. Change of plans.
Ship + Sickle	Travel bringing cancellations and course changes.
Sickle + House	Sale of house or property.
House + Sickle	Family break up, separation.
Sickle + Tree	Health, physical security, growth.
Tree + Sickle	Surgery, invasive procedure.
Sickle + Cloud	Problems with recurrent thoughts.
Cloud + Sickle	Irrational decision.
Sickle + Snake	Lack of libido, impotence.
Snake + Sickle	Betrayal provoking pain and endings.
Sickle + Coffin	Severe and recurrent disease.
Coffin + Sickle	Changes creating deep loss in a situation.
Sickle + Bouquet	Harvesting happiness, balance, success.
Bouquet + Sickle	Positive decisions. Surgery successful.
Sickle + Whip	Elimination of negative energy, magic or spell.
Whip + Sickle	Suffering, pain ending.
Sickle + Birds	End of gossip, conversation, communication.
Birds + Sickle	Arguments being enforced.
Sickle + Child	Renewal of life with elimination of old habits or addictions.
Child + Sickle	Ingenuity and immaturity reaping negative results.
Sickle + Fox	Solution of a dark situation.
Fox + Sickle	Plans and strategies working.
Sickle + Bear	Freeing yourself from oppressors.
Bear + Sickle	Protection that irritates and bothers.
Sickle + Star	Destiny being altered.
Star + Sickle	Harvest intended and expected.
Sickle + Stork	Change of plans and direction.
Stork + Sickle	Changes bringing fruition.
Sickle + Dog	Lies; loyalty ending.
Dog + Sickle	End of a friendship.

Sickle + Tower	End of introspection, isolation.
Tower + Sickle	The necessary internalization bringing results.
Sickle + Garden	Loss of harvest, cutting of what was planted.
Garden + Sickle	Negative people, bad influence.
Sickle + Mountain	End of difficulties and problems.
Mountain + Sickle	Justice being done.
Sickle + Path	End of the path. Feeling lost.
Path + Sickle	Paths fruitful.
Sickle + Rat	Eliminate worries that take away tranquillity.
Rat + Sickle	Physical or mental illness.
Sickle + Heart	Heart surgery. Loss of feelings.
Heart + Sickle	Disgust, discouragement and disillusionment.
Sickle + Ring	Marriage breakup. Divorce, termination of contract or partnership.
Ring + Sickle	Union, productive society.
Sickle + Book	End of a secret, of history, of dedication.
Book + Sickle	Productive work. Meaningful studies.
Sickle + Letter	False news or lack of news.
Letter + Sickle	Notice of disruption, termination of contract.
Sickle + Gypsy Man	Man walking out of your life, cutting ties.
Gypsy Man + Sickle	Decisive man, confident and taking the lead.
Sickle + Gypsy Woman	Woman walking out of your life, cutting ties.
Gypsy Woman + Sickle	Decisive woman, confident and taking the lead.
Sickle + Lily	Separation or unrest
Lily + Sickle	Maturity that brings positive results.
Sickle + Sun	End of success.
Sun + Sickle	Quick success without much stability.
Sickle + Moon	Loss of intuition.
Moon + Sickle	Positive cuts made by desire itself.
Sickle + Key	Cutting ties needed to find a solution.
Key + Sickle	Important, definitive decision.
Sickle + Fish	Loss of money, status, social position.
Fish + Sickle	Money that yields, investment.
Sickle +Anchor	Definitive end.
Anchor + Sickle	Security brought by planning.
Sickle + Cross	Elimination of predictable situations.
Cross + Sickle	Volunteer work.

Card 11 - The Whip

Whip + Rider	Situation or a person that comes back from the past.
Rider + Whip	Situation that repeats itself.
Whip + Clover	Insisting on the same attitudes is cause for so many problems, change is needed.
Clover + Whip	Problems are likely to persist for a while.
Whip + Ship	Insist to continue the journey.
Ship + Whip	Travel with suffering or a personal journey of suffering.
Whip + House	Another family, another family situation.
House + Whip	Family violence.
Whip + Tree	Physical pain, heavy exercise.
Tree + Whip	Long-lasting disease, recurrent disease.
Whip + Cloud	Old sadness bringing mental confusion.
Cloud + Whip	Thoughts that cause pain and suffering.
Whip + Snake	Repeated betrayal, injuries and sexual abuse.
Snake + Whip	Promiscuity and rough sex.
Whip + Coffin	Physical attack or violence.
Coffin + Whip	Pain, painful changes that happen again.
Whip + Bouquet	Precarious balance.
Bouquet + Whip	Night-time fun, hectic party.
Whip + Sickle	Suffering and/or pain ending.
Sickle + Whip	Cut negative energy, magic, spell.
Whip + Birds	Debate, much communication, many arguments.
Birds + Whip	Difficult conversations.
Whip + Child	Punishment, return of immaturity. Children's bullying.
Child + Whip	Children upset.
Whip + Fox	End of the cleverness, of selfish plans.
Fox + Whip	Situation designed to break, inflict pain and hurt.
Whip + Bear	Insistence on taking control.
Bear + Whip	Overprotection that bothers. Great spiritual protection.
Whip + Star	Positive magic which brings positive results.
Star + Whip	Spirituality in action.
Whip + Stork	Persist in the changes. Many changes.
Stork + Whip	Quick change, possibly a change with problems.
Whip + Dog	Problems with friends.
Dog + Whip	Friendship with benefits.

Whip + Tower	The paranormal, spiritual. Self-defence, self-punishment.
Tower + Whip	Hassles of the past. Spiritual persecution.
Whip + Garden	Hectic social life.
Garden + Whip	Places that bring suffering. People influencing from afar.
Whip + Mountain	Insist, look for options and use creativity to find a solution.
Mountain + Whip	Difficulty solving problems.
Whip + Path	Sorrows that will come in choices made.
Path + Whip	Many decisions to make. Many options.
Whip + Rat	Negative harmful and dark magic.
Rat + Whip	Mental and emotional exhaustion. Breaking point.
Whip + Heart	**Insistence in a romantic situation. Sex with love.**
Heart + Whip	Feeling annoyed or feeling hurt.
Whip + Ring	Physical abuse in the relationship.
Ring + Whip	Spiritual covenant. Spiritual promise.
Whip + Book	Return to your studies, persist in your studies.
Book + Whip	Magic work. Occult sciences.
Whip + Letter	Concrete threat.
Letter + Whip	News that shakes and hurts.
Whip + Gypsy Man	Persistent, active, agile, sexual man.
Gypsy Man + Whip	Man connected to spirituality. Wizard.
Whip + Gypsy Woman	Persistent, active, agile, sexual woman.
Gypsy Woman + Whip	Woman connected to spirituality. Witch.
Whip + Lily	Physical tiredness. Middle age.
Lily + Whip	Peace and tranquillity at risk.
Whip + Sun	Competition for power.
Sun + Whip	Pleasure in sex.
Whip + Moon	May indicate magic, work done, conflict.
Moon + Whip	Great magic, magic that brings results.
Whip + Key	Discussion in search of a solution.
Key + Whip	Necessary decision making.
Whip + Fish	Adversities with money.
Fish + Whip	Greed. Diversify investments.
Whip + Anchor	Disturbing situations in stability.
Anchor + Whip	Stuck in a painful situation. No change in suffering.
Whip + Cross	End of suffering, abuse and/or physical aggression.

Cross + Whip   Path with more difficulty, challenge, difficult lesson.

Card 12 - The Birds

Birds + Rider	Good changes with greater communication.
Rider + Birds	Situation growing positively.
Birds + Clover	Increase communication to overcome problems. Gossip is making life difficult.
Clover + Birds	Temporary difficulties and small problems.
Birds + Ship	Communication about travels.
Ship + Birds	Successful travel with group of people.
Birds + House	Gossip in the family.
House + Birds	Romance between the couple.
Birds + Tree	Nature. Building conversations.
Tree + Birds	Security and growth in communications.
Birds + Cloud	Complicated conversations.
Cloud + Birds	Lies and gossip.
Birds + Snake	Slander, lies.
Snake + Birds	Group sex, sex at the heart of the matter.
Birds + Coffin	Sad things that bring change.
Coffin + Birds	**Change of subject, actions different than words.**
Birds + Bouquet	Animated conversation.
Bouquet + Birds	Invitation for meeting with known people.
Birds + Sickle	Arguments being enforced.
Sickle + Birds	End of gossip, conversation, communication.
Birds + Whip	Difficult conversations.
Whip + Birds	Debate, a lot of communication, many arguments.
Birds + Child	Communication that causes growth and change.
Child + Birds	Happy, talkative **child**.
Birds + Fox	Malicious, deceptive communication.
Fox + Birds	Group planning.
Birds + Bear	Union that causes envy and jealousy in a relationship.
Bear + Birds	Person who dominates in the art of conversation.
Birds + Star	Peace, happiness, success, wellbeing.
Star + Birds	Encounter of soul mates.
Birds + Stork	Negotiating changes, talking about changes.
Stork + Birds	News that brings joy, happy change.
Birds + Dog	Friendly talk.
Dog + Birds	Friendship sincere and true, happy.

Birds + Tower	Talk about intimate things, patience, waiting.
Tower + Birds	Spiritual communication.
Birds + Garden	Communicate more, get out more, move around the world.
Garden + Birds	Romantic, happy, positive outing.
Birds + Mountain	Situation that only leads to problems.
Mountain + Birds	Difficulty in expressing and relating to oneself.
Birds + Path	Multiple good paths.
Path + Birds	Paths of partnership.
Birds + Rat	Shocking, affecting, negative discussions.
Rat + Birds	Confusion at expressing oneself, difficulty organizing thoughts.
Birds + Heart	Romance, wise love, sublime love.
Heart + Birds	Desire for perfect union, partnership.
Birds + Ring	Talk about relationship, about marriage.
Ring + Birds	A loving, communicative partner.
Birds + Book	Professional path has been found. Professional decision.
Book + Birds	Communicative work. Secret being discovered.
Birds + Letter	Communicate more clearly and often.
Letter + Birds	Happy, pleasing news, bringing together.
Birds + Gypsy Man	Gossip from or about a man.
Gypsy Man + Birds	**Communicative man, happy.**
Birds + Gypsy Woman	Gossip from or about a woman.
Gypsy Woman + Birds	Communicative woman, happy.
Birds + Lily	Long discussions. Mature discussions that bring results.
Letter 30 Lily + Birds	Peace from the wisdom of life. Union of peace.
Birds + Sun	Definitive resolution coming from conversations.
Sun + Birds	Stability of emotions and feelings.
Birds + Moon	Creative, intuitive conversations.
Moon + Birds	Conquering through partnership and communication.
Birds + Key	Socialize to find options.
Key + Birds	The solution lies in communication.
Birds + Fish	Financial speculation, illicit money.
Fish + Birds	Momentary, fleeting prosperity.
Birds + Anchor	Stable relationship. Feelings of permanent happiness.
Anchor + Birds	A confused conversation that does not evolve or result in a solution.
Birds + Cross	Difficult communication but ending a situation.

Cross + Birds   End, disruption of negotiations. Breakdown of communication.

Card 13 - The Child

Child + Rider	Immature in the way of acting and thinking.
Rider + Child	Good news bringing joy and new beginnings.
Child + Clover	Problems with children, grandchildren, nephews or nieces.
Clover + Child	Ingenuity causing problems.
Child + Ship	Travel with children.
Ship + Child	Trip to new places.
Child + House	Children, grandchildren, nephews or nieces.
House + Child	Family in a new phase, possible birth, pregnancy.
Child + Tree	New phase of stability.
Tree + Child	Good change in health. Finding a cure.
Child + Cloud	Child with attention deficit.
Cloud + Child	Concern with children, grandchildren, nephews or nieces.
Child + Snake	Agitated child, attention deficit syndrome.
Snake + Child	A malicious person who uses naive people.
Child + Coffin	End of innocence, of irresponsibility.
Coffin + Child	Possible abortion.
Child + Bouquet	Happy child. Emotional balance.
Bouquet + Child	Pure, innocent happiness.
Child + Sickle	Ingenuity, immaturity reaping negative results.
Sickle + Child	Renewal of life with elimination of old habits or addictions.
Child + Whip	Children upset.
Whip + Child	Punishment, return of immaturity. Children's bullying.
Child + Birds	Happy, talkative, but **restless child.**
Birds + Child	Communication that causes growth and change.
Child + Fox	Don't be naive in front of cunning people and liars.
Fox + Child	Inconvenient pitfalls. Acting without thinking.
Child + Bear	Child obesity. Child being overprotected.
Bear + Child	Relationship of protection between parents and children.
Child + Star	Spiritual evolution, keen intuition.
Star + Child	Guardian Angel protection.
Child + Stork	End of adolescence, beginning of adulthood.
Stork + Child	Pregnancy, birth.

Child + Dog	Feeling sincere and true. Great loyalty.
Dog + Child	Friendship and loyalty changing life. Friends from childhood.
Child + Tower	Spiritual guide.
Tower + Child	Strong and growing intuition.
Child + Garden	Great immaturity and ingenuity.
Garden + Child	Fun, joyful, exciting times.
Child + Mountain	Children with blocks, problems.
Mountain + Child	Difficulties in changing, growing, evolving.
Child + Path	Twins. Independent child.
Path + Child	Immature, naive choices.
Child + Rat	Hyperactive children.
Rat + Child	Childhood illnesses.
Child + Heart	Young person. Beginning of feelings.
Heart + Child	Love and sincerity, pure feeling.
Child + Ring	Adoption. Child partner or fostering.
Ring + Child	Strengthening of unity by children, grandchildren, nephews, nieces.
Child + Book	Studious child, curiosity. In school.
Book + Child	Professional area going through changes. Promotion.
Child + Letter	Closed child, who keeps information to themselves.
Letter + Child	Pregnancy news.
Child + Gypsy Man	Beginning of a new life for or with a man.
Gypsy Man + Child	Immature, young, inconsequential man.
Child + Gypsy Woman	Beginning of a new life for or with a woman.
Gypsy Woman + Child	Immature, young, inconsequential woman.
Child + Lily	Peaceful, calm child, who brings peace.
Lily + Child	Premature, hurried marriage.
Child + Sun	Desired, scheduled pregnancy. Restless child.
Sun + Child	Promising start. Future vision.
Child + Moon	Spiritual child.
Moon + Child	Pregnancy and birth after many attempts.
Child + Key	Phase of search for solutions.
Key + Child	Immature and childish solutions.
Child + Fish	Small amount of money coming.
Fish + Child	Materiality, prosperity growing.
Child + Anchor	New phase of security and stability.

Anchor + Child   Restrain children, grandchildren, nephews, nieces more.
Child + Cross   Difficult childhood. Child going through depression.
Cross + Child   Completion of a phase to start a new one.

Card 14 - The Fox

Fox + Rider	Trap that will require speediness for an effective solution.
Rider + Fox	Act with cunning, think of strategies to achieve goals.
Fox + Clover	Use cleverness to overcome problems.
Clover + Fox	Problems and pitfalls in the situation.
Fox + Ship	Traps coming, be careful.
Ship + Fox	Well planned trip.
Fox + House	Use cunning to acquire real estate.
House + Fox	Theft in the family, in the house.
Fox + Tree	Wrongly diagnosed disease. Seek a second opinion
Tree + Fox	Hidden disease. Physical traps.
Fox + Cloud	Mental traps.
Cloud + Fox	Doubtful character.
Fox + Snake	Traps that led to betrayal.
Snake + Fox	Great betrayal. Breach of promise.
Fox + Coffin	Use cunning and cleverness to achieve change.
Coffin + Fox	End of lies. Traps that fail.
Fox + Bouquet	Emotional trap.
Bouquet + Fox	Success at risk.
Fox + Sickle	Plans and strategies working.
Sickle + Fox	End of a dark situation.
Fox + Whip	Situation organized to break, hit, hurt.
Whip + Fox	End of the cleverness, of selfish plans.
Fox + Birds	Group planning.
Birds + Fox	Malicious, deceptive communication.
Fox + Child	Inconvenient pitfalls. Acting without thinking.
Child + Fox	Do not be naive in front of cunning people and liars.
Fox + Bear	Unreliable investments, dishonest boss.
Bear + Fox	Intrigues and falsities. Manipulative person.
Fox + Star	Successful planning.
Star + Fox	Positive spiritual influence bringing cleverness.
Fox + Stork	Gossip with the purpose of provoking intrigue.
Stork + Fox	Changes planned, well thought out, organized.
Fox + Dog	Careful with friendships. Friends influencing negatively.
Dog + Fox	False friend, self-interested.

Fox + Tower	Disbelief. Lack of faith.
Tower + Fox	Spiritual manipulation.
Fox + Garden	Event organization. Planning social ascension.
Garden + Fox	A situation that requires great cunning and planning.
Fox + Mountain	Planning obstructed, stopped.
Mountain + Fox	Trapped, lack of effective action.
Fox + Path	Alert, attention to choices.
Path + Fox	Doubtful, dangerous paths.
Fox + Rat	Doubtful character. Wrong plans.
Rat + Fox	Loss of attention, focus. Lack of clarity.
Fox + Heart	Attention with feelings, in love.
Heart + Fox	False feelings, using feelings of others for own benefit.
Fox + Ring	Alert about marriage, partnership, society.
Ring + Fox	Relationship for material gain.
Fox + Book	Mental attitude. Think smart.
Book + Fox	Plans architected in secrets.
Fox + Letter	Manipulation of information, documents, communication for someone's own benefit.
Letter + Fox	False, harmful news.
Fox + Gypsy Man	Alert for or about a man.
Gypsy Man + Fox	Astute man, intelligent, manipulative.
Fox + Gypsy Woman	Alert for or about a woman.
Gypsy Woman + Fox	Crafty, intelligent, manipulative woman.
Fox + Lily	Personality well defined, well resolved.
Lily + Fox	Use coolness and maturity in negotiations.
Fox + Sun	Pay attention to things that are obvious. Open your eyes.
Sun + Fox	Misleading, false success.
Fox + Moon	Wrong handling of spiritual things.
Moon + Fox	Disgraceful situation.
Fox + Key	Plan to find solutions.
Key + Fox	Undo traps, manipulations.
Fox + Fish	Financial trap.
Fish + Fox	Corruption, misuse of money.
Fox + Anchor	Ancient dishonesty which persists, rooted.
Anchor + Fox	Trapped.
Fox + Cross	Stuck in lies and deceit.
Cross + Fox	End of a dangerous and manipulative situation.

Card 15 - The Bear

Bear + Rider	End of domineering situation.
Rider + Bear	Get rid of fake, controlling and jealous people.
Bear + Clover	Protect yourself in the situation to solve problems.
Clover + Bear	Problems with organization and administration of the situation.
Bear + Ship	Search for distant safety.
Ship + Bear	Displacements required for self-protection.
Bear + House	Investment in real estate.
House + Bear	Protected family, which protects each other.
Bear + Tree	Manage the situation more safely.
Tree + Bear	Obesity, eating disorder
Bear + Cloud	Mental domination causing confusion.
Cloud + Bear	Fear and insecurity.
Bear + Snake	A person who likes morbid and kinky sex.
Snake + Bear	Betrayal of feelings, of affection.
Bear + Coffin	Lack of vital energy, lack of passion for life, person without strength.
Coffin + Bear	Losses and annoyances. Person passed away.
Bear + Bouquet	Balance being destroyed. Instability, feeling of pressure.
Bouquet + Bear	Support bringing safety.
Bear + Sickle	Protection that irritates and bothers.
Sickle + Bear	Freeing yourself from oppressors.
Bear + Whip	Overprotection that bothers. Great spiritual protection.
Whip + Bear	Insistence on taking control.
Bear + Birds	Person who dominates the art of conversation.
Birds + Bear	Union that causes envy. Jealousy in a relationship.
Bear + Child	Relationship of protection between parents and children.
Child + Bear	Child obesity. Child being overprotected.
Bear + Fox	Intrigues and falsities. Manipulative person.
Fox + Bear	Unreliable investments, dishonest boss.
Bear + Star	Great spiritual protection.
Star + Bear	Person or situation of spiritual strength.
Bear + Stork	Risk in pregnancy, alert with childbirth.
Stork + Bear	A situation that changes with violent discussions.
Bear + Dog	Suffocating, restrictive friend. Fake friendship.

Dog + Bear	Protective and often domineering friend.
Bear + Tower	Dominated by self, selfish thoughts.
Tower + Bear	Forced isolation.
Bear + Garden	Illusory projects that deceive.
Garden + Bear	Great protection, great domination.
Bear + Mountain	Overcoming strength problems.
Mountain + Bear	Obstacles caused by difficult temperament.
Bear + Path	Bisexuality, double passion, person divided in love life.
Path + Bear	Intelligent but selfish choices.
Bear + Rat	A malicious, selfish person who harms.
Rat + Bear	Situation of stress causing loss of control.
Bear + Heart	Feeling, false love.
Heart + Bear	Jealousy and loving possession.
Bear + Ring	Bad financial agreement.
Ring + Bear	Relationship where jealousy, fights and sexual attraction reign.
Bear + Book	Protecting secrets.
Book + Bear	Work or major studies.
Bear + Letter	Protect documents, news, what is known.
Letter + Bear	News, communication of extreme importance.
Bear + Gypsy Man	Success for a man or coming from a man.
Gypsy Man + Bear	Protective, domineering, jealous, possessive man.
Bear + Gypsy Woman	Success for a woman or coming from a woman.
Gypsy Woman + Bear	Protective, domineering, jealous, possessive woman.
Bear + Lily	Prosperity acquired during life.
Lily + Bear	Peace and lasting happiness.
Bear + Sun	Clear, visible evil.
Sun + Bear	Great prosperity, success, social elevation.
Bear + Moon	Self-protection, someone who protects, something guaranteed.
Moon + Bear	Individual progress, loneliness.
Bear + Key	Finding solutions, mastering options.
Key + Bear	Solving problems in a selfish way.
Bear + Fish	Take a breath to be able to thrive financially.
Fish + Bear	Money saved, hidden.
Bear + Anchor	Grumpy person, stuck in his/her own ideas.
Anchor + Bear	**Feeling of domination from another person.**

Bear + Cross	Still fighting for the happy ending.
Cross + Bear	Completion of something that took a long time, no return.

Card 16 - The Star

Star + Rider	Trust your own intuition to open your ways.
Rider + Star	Realization of dreams with the help of the spiritual.
Star + Clover	Overcoming problems with divine help.
Clover + Star	Spiritual problems.
Star + Ship	Astral travel. Dreams.
Ship + Star	Travel and displacement of success.
Star + House	Family achievement.
House + Star	Spiritual family. Ancestors.
Star + Tree	Physical healing.
Tree + Star	Spiritual treatment.
Star + Cloud	A situation of mental confusion that quickly dissipates.
Cloud + Star	Do not procrastinate, act. Be proactive.
Star + Snake	Quick, agile resolution taken.
Snake + Star	Feeling of spiritual betrayal, of unworthiness.
Star + Coffin	Intuition helping in times of transition.
Coffin + Star	Positive transformation.
Star + Bouquet	Hope, dreams come true.
Bouquet + Star	Perfect gift.
Star + Sickle	Harvest intended and expected.
Sickle + Star	Destiny being altered.
Star + Whip	Spirituality in action.
Whip + Star	Positive magic, which brings positive results.
Star + Birds	Encounter of soul mates.
Birds + Star	Peace, happiness, success, wellbeing.
Star + Child	Guardian Angel protection.
Child + Chart	Spiritual evolution, keen intuition.
Star + Fox	Positive spiritual influence bringing cleverness.
Fox + Star	Successful planning.
Star + Bear	Great ideas.
Bear + Star	Spiritual protection, spiritual realm.
Star + Stork	Thoughts being changed positively.
Stork + Star	Positive changes, with good results.
Star + Dog	Great loyalty from a good person.
Dog + Star	Friendship that brings luck, success.
Star + Tower	Spiritual mentors or gypsy spirits.

Tower + Star	Clairvoyance.
Star + Garden	Social brilliance, own brilliance.
Garden + Star	Spiritual event. Spiritual place.
Star + Mountain	Broken dreams.
Mountain + Star	Difficulty in accomplishing things, refusal to shine.
Star + Path	Realization in the choices.
Path + Star	Spiritual mission.
Star + Rat	Loss of morale, respect, fame.
Rat + Star	Fear of success, fame.
Star + Heart	Great passion, adoration.
Heart + Star	Relationship, love, blessed feeling.
Star + Ring	Good relationship.
Ring + Star	Successful spiritual alliance.
Star + Book	Professional success.
Book + Star	Artistic work.
Star + Letter	Spiritual communication.
Letter + Star	Letter of recommendation.
Star + Gypsy Man	Spiritual mentor or spiritual Gypsy.
Gypsy Man + Star	Spiritual man, medium. Gypsy blood.
Star + Gypsy Woman	Spiritual mentor or spiritual Gypsy.
Gypsy Woman + Star	Spiritual woman, medium. Gypsy Blood.
Star + Lily	Success that comes from the past. Old.
Lily + Star	Something that keeps fame under control, is not dazzled.
Star + Sun	Dreams come true, fame, good luck.
Sun + Star	Success and prestige.
Star + Moon	Very well-deserved success.
Moon + Star	Hide success.
Star + Key	Prize, to win things.
Key + Star	Open your own spirituality.
Star + Fish	Financial success.
Fish + Star	Prosperity, fame, success, brilliance itself.
Star + Anchor	Long-term fame.
Anchor + Star	Stuck in self.
Star + Cross	Spiritual thoughts, of faith, of God.
Cross + Star	Destiny, karma, pre-destination and soul mates.

Card 17 - The Stork

Stork + Rider	Look for new ways for the situation to change for the better.
Rider + Stork	Unexpected pregnancy.
Stork + Clover	New situation bringing problems.
Clover + Stork	Problems causing you to change course.
Stork + Ship	Air travel.
Ship + Stork	Journey to good news.
Stork + House	New house, change of residence.
House + Stork	Renovation of property. Internal changes.
Stork + Tree	Go for growth and stability.
Tree + Stork	Physical recovery.
Stork + Cloud	Search to discover, to find, to clear.
Cloud + Stork	Wrong bet, wrong choice.
Stork + Snake	Difficult change about to happen.
Snake + Stork	Route deviation.
Stork + Coffin	Boredom, monotony, lack of goals.
Coffin + Stork	Change the way you act, want and think.
Stork + Bouquet	Positive change, happy.
Bouquet + Stork	Unexpected pregnancy. Adoption.
Stork + Sickle	Changes bringing fruition.
Sickle + Stork	Change of plans and direction.
Stork + Whip	Quick change, possibly a change with problems.
Whip + Stork	Persist in the changes. Many changes.
Stork + Birds	News that brings joy, happy change.
Birds + Stork	Negotiating changes, talking about changes.
Stork + Child	Pregnancy, birth.
Child + Stork	End of adolescence, beginning of adulthood.
Stork + Fox	Changes planned, well thought out, organized.
Fox + Stork	Gossip with the purpose of provoking intrigue.
Stork + Bear	A situation that changes with violent discussions.
Bear + Stork	Risk in pregnancy, alert with childbirth.
Stork + Star	Positive changes, with good results.
Star + Stork	Thoughts being changed positively.
Stork + Dog	New friendships.
Dog + Stork	Friendship that transforms, that changes.

Stork + Tower	News about the past.
Tower + Stork	Interior changes.
Stork + Garden	Move away.
Garden + Stork	New project.
Stork + Mountain	Changes fair, sought after. Overcoming obstacles.
Mountain + Stork	Difficulties making changes, projects.
Stork + Path	Changing your mind, choices.
Path + Stork	Paths of great changes.
Stork + Rat	Sad news that hurts.
Rat + Stork	Overcoming stress.
Stork + Heart	New love, new feeling.
Heart + Stork	Willingness to change, from something new and/or unexpected.
Stork + Ring	New union, new relationship.
Ring + Stork	End of relationship, union, partnership, social circle.
Stork + Book	Professional changes, new job.
Book + Stork	Professional promotion, new studies.
Stork + Letter	News being communicated.
Letter + Stork	Formalize the changes.
Stork + Gypsy Man	Changes and news for or about a man. Pregnancy.
Gypsy Man + Stork	Flexible, open-minded man.
Stork + Gypsy Woman	Changes and news for or about a woman. Pregnancy.
Gypsy Woman + Stork	Flexible, open-minded woman.
Stork + Lily	Sentient, balanced news.
Lily + Stork	Coldness causing changes.
Stork + Sun	Pregnancy.
Sol + Stork	Positivity favouring transformations. Energy on the rise.
Stork + Moon	News sought, deserved.
Moon + Stork	Personal success sought.
Stork + Key	News that show solutions.
Key + Stork	Discovering a surprise.
Stork + Fish	Changing the financial situation.
Fish + Stork	Fast arrival of news.
Stork + Anchor	Improved safety.
Anchor + Stork	Stagnation, nothing new.
Stork + Cross	Difficult changes.
Cross + Stork	Plans changed, unwanted change.

Card 18 - The Dog

Dog + Rider	Lean on friends and their loyalty.
Rider + Dog	Loyal friends will appear with a life change.
Dog + Clover	Friends/friendship going through problems.
Clover + Dog	Troubled relationship with friends.
Dog + Ship	Distant friend.
Ship + Dog	Travel with friends.
Dog + House	Neighbours, people nearby.
House + Dog	A united and loyal family.
Dog + Tree	Twin soul, strong and true friendship.
Tree + Dog	Medical team, health professionals.
Dog + Cloud	Unreliable friend.
Cloud + Dog	Judgment wrong, not clear.
Dog + Snake	Unfaithful, false friend.
Snake + Dog	Betrayal from someone you trust.
Dog + Coffin	Friend who needs help.
Coffin + Dog	Birth of a friendship.
Dog + Bouquet	Complete, loyal, balanced friendship.
Bouquet + Dog	Gain something which awaits.
Dog + Sickle	End of a friendship.
Sickle + Dog	Lies, loyalty ending.
Dog + Whip	Friendship with benefits. Friendship with sex.
Whip + Dog	Problems with friends.
Dog + Birds	Friendship sincere and true, happy.
Birds + Dog	Friendly talk.
Dog + Child	Friendship and loyalty changing life. Friends from childhood.
Child + Dog	Feeling sincere and true. Great loyalty.
Dog + Fox	False friend, self-interested.
Fox + Dog	Careful with friendships. Friends influencing negatively.
Dog + Bear	Protective and often domineering friend.
Bear + Dog	Suffocating, restrictive friend. Fake friendship.
Dog + Star	Friendship that brings luck, success.
Star + Dog	Great loyalty from a good person.
Dog + Stork	Friendship that transforms and changes.
Stork + Dog	New friendships.

Dog + Tower	Spiritual friend.
Tower + Dog	Friendships from the past. Friend returned to your life.
Dog + Garden	Sincere loyalty.
Garden + Dog	Party, event between friends. Great friendship.
Dog + Mountain	Friends in trouble.
Mountain + Dog	Difficulties in friendship.
Dog + Path	A decisive friendship, one that makes a difference and opens doors.
Path + Dog	Choose between people you know, friends. Take a position.
Dog + Rat	Friend that worries, troublesome friend.
Rat + Dog	Friendship break, loss of a friend.
Dog + Heart	Friendship that turns to love.
Heart + Dog	A loving friendship. Emotional loyalty.
Dog + Ring	Loyalty reinforcing a union, social circle, relationship.
Ring + Dog	Partnership among friends or dating between friends.
Dog + Book	Intelligent friend.
Book + Dog	Work with friends. Studies with friends.
Dog + Letter	News, information from or for a friend.
Letter + Dog	True, correct documents.
Dog + Gypsy Man	Friends acting on behalf of a man. Male friendship.
Gypsy Man + Dog	Faithful man, friend, companion, trustworthy, cordial.
Dog + Gypsy Woman	Friends acting on behalf of a woman. Female friendship.
Gypsy Woman + Dog	Faithful woman, friend, companion, trustworthy, cordial.
Dog + Lily	Wise friend, important, from long ago.
Lily + Dog	Coldness in a friendship.
Dog + Sun	True friendship. Reciprocal friendship.
Sun + Dog	Great friendship, great loyalty.
Dog + Moon	Guides, teachers, spiritual friends.
Moon + Dog	Conquest with loyal friends.
Dog + Key	Loyalty that makes decisions, opens options.
Key + Dog	Creating new friends, expanding the circle of friends.
Dog + Fish	Financial partner, business partner.
Fish + Dog	Friendship for financial interest.
Dog + Anchor	Stable, lasting friendship.
Anchor + Dog	Feeling trapped by friendships. Stopped, not evolving.
Dog + Cross	Difficult friendship that makes you suffer, that hurts.

Cross + Dog   Overcoming and finishing something with the help of friends.

Card 19 - The Tower

Tower + Rider	Isolate for internal reassessment, for personal evolution.
Rider + Tower	End of period of solitude and depression.
Tower + Clover	Difficulty at personal and intimate level.
Clover + Tower	Spiritual problems and distancing from reality.
Tower + Ship	Journey into yourself.
Ship + Tower	Solitary journey.
Tower + House	Look at your inner self. Find balance.
House + Tower	Spiritual balance.
Tower + Tree	Individual plans.
Tree + Tower	Interior growth.
Tower + Cloud	Spiritual entities.
Cloud + Tower	Depression, mental or psychological confusion.
Tower + Snake	Negative spirit, something false.
Snake + Tower	Negative thoughts of betrayal.
Tower + Coffin	End of solitude.
Coffin + Tower	Possible death or risk of dying.
Tower + Bouquet	Balanced spirituality.
Bouquet + Tower	Be well with yourself, get out of solitude, be able to exteriorize your joy.
Tower + Sickle	The necessary internalization bringing results.
Sickle + Tower	End of introspection, isolation.
Tower + Whip	Hassles of the past. Spiritual persecution.
Whip + Tower	The paranormal, spiritual. Self-defence, self-punishment.
Tower + Birds	Spiritual communication.
Birds + Tower	Talk about intimate things, patience, waiting.
Tower + Child	Strong and growing intuition.
Child + Tower	Spiritual guide.
Tower + Fox	Spiritual manipulation.
Fox + Tower	Disbelief. Lack of faith.
Tower + Bear	Forced isolation.
Bear + Tower	Dominated by self, selfish thoughts.
Tower + Star	Clairvoyance.
Star + Tower	Spiritual mentors or Gypsy spirits.
Tower + Stork	Interior changes.
Stork + Tower	News about the past.

Tower + Dog	Friendships from the past. Friend returned to your life.
Dog + Tower	Spiritual friend.
Tower + Garden	Social isolation, lack of social commitment.
Garden + Tower	Distant relatives or acquaintances.
Tower + Mountain	Solitude that hinders. Spiritual shock.
Mountain + Tower	Delayed justice. Unique problems. Difficulty meeting.
Tower + Path	Spirituality acting in life.
Path + Tower	Lonely way, following alone.
Tower + Rat	Loyalty broken, unstructured.
Rat + Tower	Stress that comes from far, ancient.
Tower + Heart	The emotional interior. The loneliness of love.
Heart + Tower	Feelings of exclusion, abandonment.
Tower + Ring	Distant, lonely relationship.
Ring + Tower	Relationship, union, old society. Connection with the spiritual.
Tower + Book	Work and studies related to the spiritual.
Book + Tower	Secrets of the past.
Tower + Letter	Spiritual or past warnings.
Letter + Tower	Old documents. Unique documents.
Tower + Gypsy Man	Man from the past.
Gypsy Man + Tower	Lonely man, arrogant, spiritual.
Tower + Gypsy Woman	Woman from the past.
Gypsy Woman + Tower	Lonely woman, arrogant, spiritual.
Tower + Lily	Inner peace, peace with yourself.
Lily + Tower	Spiritual wisdom.
Tower + Sun	Solitude that brings personal evolution.
Sun + Tower	Ancient spirituality, of other lives, of birth.
Tower + Moon	Emotional internalization to find ways to achieve things.
Moon + Tower	Solo achievements, only yours.
Tower + Key	Seek the solutions in the past.
Key + Tower	Changing the solitary phase, opening options to relate.
Tower + Fish	Spirituality is being used for financial purposes.
Fish + Tower	Great solitude and detachment.
Tower + Anchor	Stuck in self-imposed solitude.
Anchor + Tower	Spiritual security.
Tower + Cross	Religious site, temple, church, centre.
Cross + Tower	Decision, choice, struggle for isolation, for loneliness.

Card 20 - The Garden

Garden + Rider	Socialize.
Rider + Garden	Period of peace, tranquillity and concretization arriving.
Garden + Clover	Social relationships with problems.
Clover + Garden	Several small problems in social relationships.
Garden + Ship	Party, socialization outside the comfort zone.
Ship + Garden	Long journey.
Garden + House	Keep a certain distance from the family.
House + Garden	Large and/or dispersed family.
Garden + Tree	Social security.
Tree + Garden	Linked to nature, to seek nature.
Garden + Cloud	Magnification of confused thoughts.
Cloud + Garden	Uncertainty in projects.
Garden + Snake	Lack of social interaction.
Snake + Garden	A person who stands out in physical appearance.
Garden + Coffin	Changes brought about by external events. Lack of control.
Coffin + Garden	Social event cancellation. End of a social relationship.
Garden + Bouquet	Successful social event.
Bouquet + Garden	Great balance, happiness.
Garden + Sickle	**Meeting new people, but bad influence.**
Sickle + Garden	Loss of harvest, cutting of what was planted.
Garden + Whip	Places that bring suffering. People influencing from afar.
Whip + Garden	Hectic social life.
Garden + Birds	Romantic, happy, positive outing.
Birds + Garden	Communicate more, get out more, and move around the world.
Garden + Child	Fun, joyful, exciting times.
Child + Garden	Great immaturity and ingenuity.
Garden + Fox	A situation that requires great cunning and planning.
Fox + Garden	Event organization. Planning social ascension.
Garden + Bear	Great protection, great domination.
Bear + Garden	Illusory projects that deceive.
Garden + Star	Spiritual event. Spiritual place.
Star + Garden	Social brilliance, own brilliance.

Garden + Stork	New project.
Stork + Garden	Move away.
Garden + Dog	Party, event between friends. Great friendship.
Dog + Garden	Sincere loyalty.
Garden + Tower	Distant relatives. Acquaintances.
Tower + Garden	Social isolation, lack of social commitment.
Garden + Mountain	Boring, tiring social gathering. Disruptive social life.
Mountain + Garden	Change of plans. Cancellation of social event.
Garden + Path	Many options to decide.
Path + Garden	Decision on plans and projects.
Garden + Rat	Wrong decision or plan that brings pain.
Rat + Garden	Change in plans.
Garden + Heart	Magnification of feelings.
Heart + Garden	Charity.
Garden + Ring	Expansion of union, relationship. A new emotional step.
Ring + Garden	New society, union, partnership.
Garden + Book	Expansion of studies.
Book + Garden	Charity work, for the benefit of society. Social work.
Garden + Letter	Invitation to a public event, a big party.
Letter + Garden	Business, official documents.
Garden + Gypsy Man	Plans made with a man.
Gypsy Man + Garden	Public, sociable, popular man.
Garden + Gypsy Woman	Plans made with a woman.
Gypsy Woman + Garden	Public, sociable, popular woman.
Garden + Lily	Safe, reliable, mature plans.
Lily + Garden	Coldness and social distancing.
Garden + Sun	Great success, magnification of positivity.
Sun + Garden	Public success. Social highlight.
Garden + Moon	Mystic event.
Moon + Garden	Social recognition.
Garden + Key	Heal through alternative medicine.
Key + Garden	Discoveries with solutions.
Garden + Fish	Magnification of materiality. Increase of customers.
Fish + Garden	Growth, enlargement, progress.
Garden + Anchor	Extending security.
Anchor + Garden	Stability and social tranquillity.
Garden + Cross	Group based on faith, spiritual, social aid.

Cross + Garden   Completion of projects and plans.

Card 21 - The Mountain

Mountain + Rider	Quick overcoming of energy consuming problems.
Rider + Mountain	Complicated phase coming. Do not run away, face it.
Mountain + Clover	Big and small problems.
Clover + Mountain	Problems of all kinds.
Mountain + Ship	Problems changing slowly.
Ship + Mountain	Journey with difficulties.
Mountain + Home	Problems being brought home.
House + Mountain	Family in trouble.
Mountain + Tree	Fatigue and insecurity.
Tree + Mountain	Serious health problems.
Mountain + Cloud	Indecision with a problematic situation.
Cloud + Mountain	Confused thoughts about problems.
Mountain + Snake	**Problems caused by betrayal.**
Snake + Mountain	Powerful foe promoting betrayals.
Mountain + Coffin	Definitive solution of problems.
Coffin + Mountain	Unfair changes, problematic.
Mountain + Bouquet	Difficulties and emotional problems. Imbalance, instability.
Bouquet + Mountain	Happiness that takes time to happen. Difficult balance.
Mountain + Sickle	Justice being done.
Sickle + Mountain	End of difficulties and problems.
Mountain + Whip	Difficulty solving problems.
Whip + Mountain	Insist, look for options, use creativity to find a solution.
Mountain + Birds	Difficulty in expressing oneself.
Birds + Mountain	Situation that only leads to problems.
Mountain + Child	Difficulties in changing, growing, evolving.
Child + Mountain	Children with blocks, problems.
Mountain + Fox	Trapped, lack of effective action.
Fox + Mountain	Planning obstructed, stopped.
Mountain + Bear	Obstacles caused by difficult temperament.
Bear + Mountain	**Overcoming strength problems.**
Mountain + Star	**Difficulty in accomplishing things, refusal to shine.**
Star + Mountain	Broken dreams.
Mountain + Stork	Difficulties making changes, projects.
Stork + Mountain	Changes fair, sought after. Overcoming obstacles.

Mountain + Dog	Difficulties in friendship.
Dog + Mountain	Friends in trouble.
Mountain + Tower	Delayed justice. Unique problems. Difficulty meeting.
Tower + Mountain	Solitude that hinders. Spiritual shock.
Mountain + Garden	Difficulty of socialization.
Garden + Mountain	Boring, tiring social gathering. Disruptive social life.
Mountain + Path	Justice on the way.
Path + Mountain	Difficulty of choices.
Mountain + Rat	Problems and difficulties bringing anxiety.
Rat + Mountain	Abominations with justice.
Mountain + Heart	Difficulties in love, sentimental, emotional.
Heart + Mountain	Feelings blocked, heart hardened.
Mountain + Ring	Complications in unions, relationships.
Ring + Mountain	Lonely, unhappy, complicated relationship.
Mountain + Book	Professional problems at work.
Book + Mountain	Knowing the difficulties.
Mountain + Letter	Delay in news, in documentation.
Letter + Mountain	**Documents, wrong commitments.**
Mountain + Gypsy Man	Problems and difficulties with a man.
Gypsy Man + Mountain	Difficult man, cold, indifferent.
Mountain + Gypsy Woman	Problems and difficulties with a woman.
Gypsy Woman + Mountain	Difficult woman, cold, indifferent.
Mountain + Lily	Lack of wisdom, of sexual life, of peace.
Lily + Mountain	**Isolation to find wisdom and justice.**
Mountain + Sun	Success happens, despite problems.
Sun + Mountain	Face your problems.
Mountain + Moon	Hidden enemy. Confusion and fears.
Moon + Mountain	Problems to get what you deserve.
Mountain + Key	Problems in the solutions found.
Key + Mountain	Overcoming and solving difficulties.
Mountain + Fish	Financial and material problems.
Fish + Mountain	Prosperity that takes time to happen.
Mountain + Anchor	Obstacles that linger.
Anchor + Mountain	Security will help overcome difficulties.
Mountain + Cross	Deep depression.
Cross + Mountain	More problems after resolving the current situation.

Card 22 - The Path

Path + Rider	The choice was made in the right way, wait for good news.
Rider + Path	More than one path to choose in a situation.
Path + Clover	Paths full of problems.
Clover + Path	Difficulties to choose.
Path + Ship	More than one option of places to choose from.
Ship + Path	Travel by land.
Path + House	Search for new family courses.
House + Path	Distant property, new location.
Path + Tree	Change of life in search of security.
Tree + Path	Branching path options.
Path + Cloud	Indecision, confusing paths, unclear options.
Cloud + Path	Great mental confusion.
Path + Snake	Path with many twists and turns, dubious ways.
Snake + Path	**Escape, a person who hides, someone low in spirit.**
Path + Coffin	End of the road, paths closed, there are no options.
Coffin + Path	More than one way to change, choice of change to make
Path + Bouquet	Correct choice of course of life.
Bouquet + Path	Good opportunities in all areas.
Path + Sickle	Paths fruitful.
Sickle + Path	End of the path. Feeling lost.
Path + Whip	Many decisions to make. Many options.
Whip + Path	Sorrows that will come in choices made.
Path + Birds	Paths of partnership.
Birds + Path	Multiple good paths.
Path + Child	Immature, naive choices.
Child + Path	Twins. Independent child.
Path + Fox	Doubtful, dangerous paths.
Fox + Path	Alert, attention to choices.
Path + Bear	Intelligent but selfish choices.
Bear + Path	Bisexuality, double passion, person divided in love life.
Path + Star	Spiritual mission.
Star + Path	Realization in the choices.
Path + Stork	Paths of great changes.
Stork + Path	Changing your mind, choices.

Path + Dog	Choose between people you know, friends. Take a position.
Dog + Path	A decisive friendship, one that makes difference and opens doors.
Path + Tower	Lonely way, to follow alone.
Tower + Path	Spirituality acting in life.
Path + Garden	Decision on plans and projects.
Garden + Path	Many options to decide.
Path + Mountain	Difficulty of choices.
Mountain + Path	Justice on the way.
Path + Rat	Complicated options and paths. Difficult choices.
Rat + Path	**A person is becoming nervous by choice.**
Path + Heart	Harmony on the path or new love.
Heart + Path	Various forms of family love, of friends, of companion.
Path + Ring	New societies, union, relationship.
Ring + Path	More of a union, partnership, relationship.
Path + Book	New professional and study options.
Book + Path	Study the options better. Discover new paths.
Path + Letter	Legal matters.
Letter + Path	News on the way. Documents being prepared.
Path + Gypsy Man	Options with a man.
Gypsy Man + Path	Man indecisive, unstable, hesitant.
Path + Gypsy Woman	Options with a woman.
Gypsy Woman + Path	Woman indecisive, unsteady, hesitant.
Path + Lily	Paths of peace, tranquillity and maturity.
Lily + Path	Stay cool to decide. Use wisdom to decide.
Path + Sun	Correct, successful choices.
Sun + Path	Great event.
Path + Moon	Decisions based on the emotional side.
Moon + Path	**Deserved and relaxed path.**
Path + Key	Various means of solving, various solutions.
Key + Path	Solution or path opening. Open to the public.
Path + Fish	Paths of prosperity.
Fish + Path	Money entering through more than one source.
Path + Anchor	Decisions taken safely.
Anchor + Path	Locked in options, choices.
Path + Cross	Destiny.

Cross + Path   Difficulty to choose, to walk, to act.

Card 23 - The Rat

Rat + Rider	A stressful situation will change quickly, bringing news.
Rider + Rat	Beware of a person/situation consuming your energy.
Rat + Clover	Mental stress bringing problems.
Clover + Rat	Stressful, mental problems.
Rat + Ship	Wait for the right time to travel or to move.
Ship + Rat	Confusing journey causing stress.
Rat + House	Stress affecting the family.
House + Rat	Family relationship worn.
Rat + Tree	General health problems. Check-up needed.
Tree + Rat	Nervous and stress getting deeper.
Rat + Cloud	Stress causing worries and sorrows.
Cloud + Rat	Mental confusion that corrodes, destroys, stresses.
Rat + Snake	Anxiety, lost person, suffering.
Snake + Rat	Great worsening of confusion.
Rat + Coffin	Big losses.
Coffin + Rat	Change of stressful situation.
Rat + Bouquet	**Lack of balance, fears and unhappiness.**
Bouquet + Rat	Unpleasant surprises.
Rat + Sickle	Physical or mental illness.
Sickle + Rat	Cut of worries that take away the tranquillity.
Rat + Whip	Mental and emotional exhaustion. Breaking point.
Whip + Rat	Negative harmful and dark magic.
Rat + Birds	Confusion at expressing oneself, difficulty organizing thoughts.
Birds + Rat	Shocking, affecting, negative discussions.
Rat + Child	Childhood illnesses.
Child + Rat	Hyperactive children.
Rat + Fox	Loss of attention, focus. Lack of clarity.
Fox + Rat	Doubtful character. Wrong plans.
Rat + Bear	Situation of stress causing loss of control.
Bear + Rat	A malicious, selfish person who harms.
Rat + Star	Fear of success, fame.
Star + Rat	Loss of morale, respect, fame.
Rat + Stork	Overcoming stress.
Stork + Rat	Sad news that hurts.

Rat + Dog	Friendship break, loss of a friend.
Dog + Rat	Friend that worries, troublesome friend.
Rat + Tower	Stress that comes from far, ancient.
Tower + Rat	Loyalty broken, unstructured.
Rat + Garden	Change in planning, in plans.
Garden + Rat	**Wrong decision or plan that brings pain.**
Rat + Mountain	Abominations with justice.
Mountain + Rat	Problems and difficulties bringing anxiety.
Rat + Path	A person who is becoming **nervous by choice.**
Path + Rat	Complicated options and paths. Difficult choices.
Rat + Heart	Emotional exhaustion.
Heart + Rat	Destructive, bad feelings.
Rat + Ring	You wear out in a union, relationship, partnership, your social circle
Ring + Rat	Stressful, complicated relationship.
Rat + Book	Emotional and mental problems with professional life.
Book + Rat	Weary work.
Rat + Letter	Lack of news, misplaced correspondence, loss of documents.
Letter + Rat	News or complicated documents, which bring harm.
Rat + Gypsy Man	Weariness or theft from or provoked by a man.
Gypsy Man + Rat	Exhausted, tired, depressed man.
Rat + Gypsy Woman	Weariness or theft from or provoked by a woman.
Gypsy Woman + Rat	Woman exhausted, tired, depressed.
Rat + Lily	End of an unofficial relationship.
Lily + Rat	Problems for an elderly person.
Rat + Sun	Loss of energy, anaemia, weakness, illness.
Sun + Rat	Great annoyance.
Rat + Moon	Depression, insecurity, insomnia.
Moon + Rat	Fraudulent achievements.
Rat + Key	Struggling to find solutions.
Key + Rat	Search useless, negative.
Rat + Fish	Theft of money, goods.
Fish + Rat	Illicit money, conquered in the wrong way.
Rat + Anchor	Lack of balance and safety.
Anchor + Rat	The stress is becoming more and more.
Rat + Cross	Deep weariness in faith.

Cross + Rat   Great loss.

Card 24 - The Heart

Heart + Rider	New love, new feelings, new emotional paths.
Rider + Heart	Emotional news coming, bringing joy and security
Heart + Clover	Feelings causing problems.
Clover + Heart	Emotional problems.
Heart + Ship	Distant feelings, feelings ending.
Ship + Heart	Emotional, sentimental journey.
Heart + House	Loving and emotional family.
Home + Heart	Emotional balance of the person.
Heart + Tree	Emotions creating roots.
Tree + Heart	Magnification of feelings. Heart problems.
Heart + Cloud	Conflicting feelings.
Cloud + Heart	Indecision in love.
Heart + Snake	Feeling of revenge.
Snake + Heart	Hatred.
Heart + Coffin	Feelings and emotions calling for radical changes.
Coffin + Heart	End of feelings, dislike of something or someone.
Heart + Bouquet	Feelings of happiness, balance, success.
Bouquet + Heart	Happiness in love.
Heart + Sickle	Disgust, discouragement, disillusionment.
Sickle + Heart	Heart surgery. **Loss of feelings**.
Heart + Whip	Feeling annoyed or feeling hurt.
Whip + Heart	Insisting on love. Sex with love.
Heart + Birds	Desire for perfect union, partnership.
Birds + Heart	Romance, wise love, sublime love.
Heart + Child	Love and sincerity, pure feeling.
Child + Heart	Young person. Beginning of feelings.
Heart + Fox	False feelings, using the feelings of others for own benefit.
Fox + Heart	Attention with feelings, in love.
Heart + Bear	Jealousy and loving possession.
Bear + Heart	Feeling, false love.
Heart + Star	Relationship, love, blessed feeling.
Star + Heart	Great passion, adoration.
Heart + Stork	Willingness to change, from something new and/or unexpected.

Stork + Heart	New love, new feeling.
Heart + Dog	A loving friendship. Emotional loyalty.
Dog + Heart	Friendship that turns to love.
Heart + Tower	Feelings of exclusion, abandonment.
Tower + Heart	The emotional interior. The loneliness of love.
Heart + Garden	Charity.
Garden + Heart	Magnification of feelings.
Heart + Mountain	Feelings blocked, heart hardened.
Mountain + Heart	Difficulties in love, sentimental, emotional.
Heart + Path	Various forms of family love, of friends, of companion.
Path + Heart	Harmony on the path or new love.
Heart + Rat	Destructive, bad feelings.
Rat + Heart	Emotional exhaustion.
Heart + Ring	Arrival of something emotional into the relationship. Marriage.
Ring + Heart	Relationship, union, partnership based on feelings.
Heart + Book	Dedication and professional commitment, with work and/or studies.
Book + Heart	Passionate work.
Heart + Letter	Feelings being declared, assumed.
Letter + Heart	News that will thrill.
Heart + Gypsy Man	Feelings from a man.
Gypsy Man + Heart	Man in love, emotional, sentimental.
Heart + Gypsy Woman	Feelings from a woman.
Gypsy Woman + Heart	Woman in love, emotional, sentimental.
Heart + Lily	Cold and calculating feelings.
Lily + Heart	Emotional maturity.
Heart + Sun	**Feelings that cannot be avoided, true love.**
Sun + Heart	Sexual romance, new love, passion.
Heart + Moon	Romance that can turn into something lasting.
Moon + Heart	Feelings hidden, guarded.
Heart + Key	Someone will open their heart, feelings will be revealed.
Key + Heart	Emotional Solutions.
Heart + Fish	Material and financial satisfaction.
Fish + Heart	Person or materialistic situation, attached to money.
Heart + Anchor	Deep and secure feelings.
Anchor + Heart	Emotional prison.

Heart + Cross   Faith in every way.
Cross + Heart   End of a feeling, of an emotion.

Card 25 - The Ring

Ring + Rider	Alliances that were formed bringing a new phase of joy and stability.
Rider + Ring	Good period coming from alliances in every way, enjoy.
Ring + Clover	This alliance will bring trouble.
Clover + Ring	Relationship problems.
Ring + Ship	Travel after formalized alliance.
Ship + Ring	Travel with partner.
Ring + House	Buy, sell or rent property.
House + Ring	Marriage, stable situation, family constitution.
Ring + Tree	A new alliance bringing stability.
Tree + Ring	Relation stable and secure. Long-term agreement.
Ring + Cloud	Problematic alliance, uncertain contracts.
Cloud + Ring	Relationship problems, lack of clarity and common vision.
Ring + Snake	Intense relationship.
Snake + Ring	Marital betrayal.
Ring + Coffin	Transformative Alliance.
Coffin + Ring	Separation, divorce.
Ring + Bouquet	Happy marriage, union with happiness.
Bouquet + Ring	Soul mate, happiness and union.
Ring + Sickle	Union, productive society.
Sickle + Ring	Marriage breakup. Divorce, termination of contract and end of a partnership.
Ring + Whip	Spiritual Covenant. Spiritual promise.
Whip + Ring	Physical abuse in the relationship.
Ring + Birds	A loving, communicative partner.
Birds + Ring	Talk about relationship, about marriage.
Ring + Child	Strengthening of unity by children, grandchildren, nephews, nieces.
Child + Ring	Adoption. Child partner or fostering.
Ring + Fox	Relationship for material gain.
Fox + Ring	Alert about marriage, partnership, society.
Ring + Bear	Relationship where jealousy, fights and sexual attraction reign.
Bear + Ring	Bad financial agreement.

Ring + Star	Successful spiritual alliance.
Star + Ring	Good relationship.
Ring + Stork	End of relationship, union, partnership, social circle.
Stork + Ring	New union, new relationship.
Ring + Dog	Partnership among friends or dating between friends.
Dog + Ring	Loyalty reinforcing a union, social circle, relationship.
Ring + Tower	Relationship, union, old society. Connection with the spiritual.
Tower + Ring	Distant and lonely relationship.
Ring + Garden	New society, union, partnership.
Garden + Ring	Expansion of union, relationship. A new emotional step.
Ring + Mountain	Lonely, unhappy, complicated relationship.
Mountain + Ring	Complications in unions, relationships.
Ring + Path	More of a union, partnership, relationship.
Path + Ring	New partnership, union, relationship.
Ring + Rat	Stressful, complicated relationship.
Rat + Ring	You wear out in a union, relationship, partnership, your social circle.
Ring + Heart	Relationship, union, partnership based on feelings.
Heart + Ring	Arrival of something emotional into the relationship. Marriage.
Ring + Book	Professional relationship. Partner, society.
Book + Ring	Study better relationships, societies, partnerships.
Ring + Letter	Written agreement. Legal matters.
Letter + Ring	News from the partner, partnership, society, union.
Ring + Gypsy Man	Union, society, partnership with a man.
Gypsy Man + Ring	Married, committed man.
Ring + Gypsy Woman	Union, society, partnership with a woman.
Gypsy Woman + Ring	Married, committed woman.
Ring + Lily	Serious, mature relationship.
Lily + Ring	Coldness in marriage, partnership, relationship.
Ring + Sun	Partnership, relationship, successful union.
Sun + Ring	Next step in the relationship.
Ring + Moon	Union, agreement, successful social circle.
Moon + Ring	Emotional, spiritual, strong connection.
Ring + Key	Agreement made, relationship official.
Key + Ring	Solve the union, the relationship, the society.
Ring + Fish	Financial, material relationship.

Fish + Ring	Prosperity bringing unity.
Ring + Anchor	Stable, secure, old relationship.
Anchor + Ring	Feeling pressured in an engagement.
Ring + Cross	Difficult relationship.
Cross + Ring	End of a relationship after much suffering.

Card 26 - The Book

Book + Rider	Keep details of plans, projects, work and studies to yourself.
Rider + Book	Take advantage of the opportunities that will arise from new work and study.
Book + Clover	Troubled secrets.
Clover + Book	Educational and professional problems.
Book + Ship	New job, position, professional opportunity coming.
Ship + Book	Professional or study related travel.
Book + Home	Home office, work from home.
House + Book	Family business and work with a relative.
Book + Tree	Keep plans for growth a secret.
Tree + Book	Disease that has not yet been detected.
Book + Cloud	Confused professional period.
Cloud + Book	Secrets bringing sorrow and confusion.
Book + Snake	Unpleasant secret. Professional betrayal.
Snake + Book	Secret Lover. Hidden sexual desire.
Book + Coffin	Knowledge bringing about a radical change. Secret revealed.
Coffin + Book	Change of work field, profession, studies.
Book + Bouquet	Successful studies, great learning.
Bouquet + Book	Professional balance.
Book + Sickle	Productive work. Studies well used.
Sickle + Book	End of the secret, of history, of dedication.
Book + Whip	Magic work. Occult sciences.
Whip + Book	Return to your studies, persist in your studies.
Book + Birds	Communicative work. Secret being discovered.
Birds + Book	Professional path has been found. Professional decision.
Book + Child	Professional area undergoing changes. Promotion.
Child + Book	Studious child, curiosity. In school.
Book + Fox	Plans architected in secrets.
Fox + Book	Mental attitude. Smart person.
Book + Bear	Work or major studies.
Bear + Book	Protecting secrets.
Book + Star	Artistic work.

Star + Book	Professional success.
Book + Stork	Professional promotion, new studies.
Stork + Book	Professional changes, new employment.
Book + Dog	Work with friends. Studies with friends.
Dog + Book	Intelligent friend.
Book + Tower	Secrets of the past.
Tower + Book	Work and studies related to the spiritual.
Book + Garden	Charity work, for the benefit of society. Social work.
Garden + Book	Expansion of studies.
Book + Mountain	Knowing the difficulties.
Mountain + Book	Professional problems at work.
Book + Path	Study the options better. Discover new paths.
Path + Book	New professional and student options.
Book + Rat	Weary work.
Rat + Book	Emotional and mental problems with professional life.
Book + Heart	Passionate work.
Heart + Book	Dedication and professional commitment, with work and/or studies.
Book + Ring	Study better the relationships, people and partnerships.
Ring + Book	Professional relationship. Partner, society.
Book + Letter	Work with documents.
Letter + Book	Professional documents. Developing documents.
Book + Gypsy Man	Secrets coming from a man.
Gypsy Man + Book	Studious man, intelligent, dedicated, revealing.
Book + Gypsy Woman	Secrets coming from a woman.
Gypsy Woman + Book	Studious woman, intelligent, dedicated, revealing.
Book + Lily	Ancient secrets.
Lily + Book	Expert in your professional field.
Book + Sun	Professional success. Important studies.
Sun + Book	Secrets coming to the surface, being discovered.
Book + Moon	Secret, hidden.
Moon + Book	Professional promotion. Growth coming from studies.
Book + Key	Secret revealed.
Key + Book	Professional solutions.
Book + Fish	Well paid job.
Fish + Book	Investment in the professional life or in studies.
Book + Anchor	Well guarded secret, difficult to discover.

Anchor + Book   Professional Security.
Book + Cross   Studies or religious work.
Cross + Book   Difficulty to keep a secret, a burden that hurts.

Card 27 - The Letter

Letter + Rider	Take all you know, news you have received and give direction to your life.
Rider + Letter	Wait for news that will quickly move your life.
Letter + Clover	News of problems.
Clover + Letter	Difficulties with documents. Difficulty in communicating.
Letter + Ship	Invitations to travel.
Ship + Letter	Departure in search of information, documents. Changes in solutions.
Letter + House	News for the family.
House + Letter	Family documents, inventory, testament.
Letter + Tree	News of growth and stability.
Tree + Letter	Medical examination, the result of health examinations.
Letter + Cloud	Confusing news, lacking in truth.
Cloud + Letter	Difficulty of communication.
Letter + Snake	Unpleasant news.
Snake + Letter	Betrayal coming out, being discovered.
Letter + Coffin	Lost message, lack of communication.
Coffin + Letter	Radical change in the way you communicate.
Letter + Bouquet	Invitation or surprising news with a happy result.
Bouquet + Letter	Positive solution related to documents, paperwork.
Letter + Sickle	Notice of disruption, termination of contract.
Sickle + Letter	**Bad news or lack of news.**
Letter + Whipping	News that shakes, hurts.
Whip + Letter	Serious threat.
Letter + Birds	Happy, pleasing news, bringing people together.
Birds + Letter	Communicate more clearly and often.
Letter + Child	Pregnancy news.
Child + Letter	Closed child, who keeps information to themselves.
Letter + Fox	False, harmful news.
Fox + Letter	Manipulation of information, documents, communication for someone's own benefit.
Letter + Bear	News, communication of extreme importance.
Bear + Letter	Protect documents, news, what is known.
Letter + Star	Letter of recommendation, indication.

Star + Letter	Spiritual communication.
Letter + Stork	Formalize the changes.
Stork + Letter	News being communicated.
Letter + Dog	True, correct documents.
Dog + Letter	News, information from or for a friend.
Letter + Tower	Old documents. Unique documents.
Tower + Letter	Spiritual or past warnings.
Letter + Garden	Business, official documents.
Garden + Letter	Invitation to a public event, a big party.
Letter + Mountain	**Documents, wrong commitments.**
Mountain + Letter	Delay in news, in documentation.
Letter + Path	News on the way. Documents being prepared.
Path + Letter	Official matters.
Letter + Rat	News or complicated documents, which bring harm.
Rat + Letter	Lack of news, misplaced correspondence, loss of documents.
Letter + Heart	News that will thrill.
Heart + Letter	Feelings being declared.
Letter + Ring	News from the partner, partnership, society, union.
Ring + Letter	Written agreement. Company documents.
Letter + Book	Professional documents. Developing documents.
Book + Letter	Work with documents.
Letter + Gypsy Man	Notice, message, communication from a man.
Gypsy Man + Letter	Communicative man.
Letter + Gypsy Woman	Notice, message, communication from a woman.
Gypsy Woman + Letter	Communicative woman.
Letter + Lily	Old documents or old information.
Lily + Letter	Use wisdom with documents, warnings, messages.
Letter + Sun	Documents that solve issues, bring success.
Sun + Letter	Great and good news.
Letter + Moon	Message, communication, warning, anonymous news.
Moon + Letter	Official success, disclosed.
Letter + Key	Notice of something being solved.
Key + Letter	Solutions are in communications, warnings and documents.
Letter + Fish	Financial documents. Bank account.
Fish + Letter settlement..	Prosperity where documents are involved, inheritance or

Letter + Anchor	Safe and reliable notices.
Anchor + Letter	Stagnation waiting for documents.
Letter + Cross	Spiritual notice.
Cross + Letter	Finalization of documentation that took a long time.

Card 28 - The Gypsy Man

Gypsy Man + Rider	Always a man close to you, possibly a relative.
Rider + Gypsy Man	Dynamic man, agile, courageous, full of ideas and attitudes.
Gypsy Man + Clover	Man in trouble.
Clover + Gypsy Man	Difficulties with a man.
Gypsy Man + Ship	A distant man, coming slowly.
Ship + Gypsy Man	Displacement for or with a man.
Gypsy Man + House	Father, grandfather, uncle, master of the house.
House + Gypsy Man	Balanced man, structured.
Gypsy Man + Tree	Man who heals, doctor, connected to medical area.
Tree + Gypsy Man	Sick man. Physical, emotional and spiritual diseases.
Gypsy Man + Cloud	Unstable man, confused, indecisive.
Cloud + Gypsy Man	Man who hides his true self, fake.
Gypsy Man + Snake	Seductive, sensual and sexual man.
Snake + Gypsy Man	Betrayal by a man.
Gypsy Man + Coffin	Sick man, depressed, dissatisfied, cheater.
Coffin + Gypsy Man	Changes and transformations for or in a man.
Gypsy Man + Bouquet	Handsome, happy and attractive man.
Bouquet + Gypsy Man	Happiness, success, balance from a man.
Gypsy Man + Sickle	Decisive man, he is confident and takes the lead.
Sickle + Gypsy Man	Man walking out of your life, cutting ties.
Gypsy Man + Whip	Man connected to spirituality. Wizard.
Whip + Gypsy Man	Persistent, active, agile, sexual man.
Gypsy Man + Birds	Communicative man, happy, agitated.
Birds + Gypsy Man	Gossip from or about a man.
Gypsy Man + Child	Immature, young, inconsequential man.
Child + Gypsy Man	Beginning of a new life with a man.
Gypsy Man + Fox	Astute man, intelligent, manipulative.
Fox + Gypsy Man	Alert for or about a man.
Gypsy Man + Bear	Protective, domineering, jealous, possessive man.
Bear + Gypsy Man	Success for a man or coming from a man.
Gypsy Man + Star	Spiritualized man, medium. Gypsy blood.
Star + Gypsy Man	Spiritual mentor or spiritual gypsy.
Gypsy Man + Stork	Flexible, open-minded man.
Stork + Gypsy Man	Changes and news for or about a man. Pregnancy.

Gypsy Man + Dog	Faithful man, friend, companion, trustworthy, cordial.
Dog + Gypsy Man	Friends acting on behalf of a man. Male friendship.
Gypsy Man + Tower	Lonely man, arrogant, spiritual.
Tower + Gypsy Man	Man from the past.
Gypsy Man + Garden	Public, sociable, popular man.
Garden + Gypsy Man	Plans made with a man.
Gypsy Man + Mountain	Difficult man, cold, indifferent.
Mountain + Gypsy Man	Problems and difficulties for or with a man.
Gypsy Man + Path	Indecisive man, unstable, hesitant.
Path + Gypsy Man	Options for or with a man.
Gypsy Man + Rat	Exhausted, tired, depressed man. Thief.
Rat + Gypsy Man	Weariness or theft from or provoked by a man.
Gypsy Man + Heart	Man in love, emotional, sentimental.
Heart + Gypsy Man	Feelings by or from a man.
Gypsy Man + Ring	Married, committed man.
Ring + Gypsy Man	Union, society, partnership with one man.
Gypsy Man + Book	Studious man, intelligent, dedicated, revealing.
Book + Gypsy Man	Secrets about or coming from a man.
Gypsy Man + Letter	Communicative man.
Letter + Gypsy Man	Notice, message, communication from a man.
Gypsy Man + Woman	Man with a feminine personality.
Gypsy Woman + Man	A relationship, proposal on the way.
Gypsy Man + Lily	Mature, elderly, quiet, patient man.
Lily + Gypsy Man	Peace, tranquillity, retirement coming to a man.
Gypsy Man + Sun	Successful, progressive, healthy man.
Sun + Gypsy Man	Successful man in all aspects.
Gypsy Man + Moon	Creative man, intuitive, mysterious, spiritual.
Moon + Gypsy Man	Achievements for, with or of a man.
Gypsy Man + Key	Reliable man who solves problems.
Key + Gypsy Man	Solutions coming from or for a man.
Gypsy Man + Fish	Man of financial success, prosperous. Materialistic man.
Fish + Gypsy Man	Financial prosperity for a man.
Gypsy Man + Anchor	A reliable, stable man who takes time to act.
Anchor + Gypsy Man	Security with or for a man.
Gypsy Man + Cross	Religious man, overwhelmed or one who is suffering.
Cross + Gypsy Man	Delayed completion for a man.

Card 29 - The Gypsy Woman

Gypsy Woman + Rider	A woman who is always present, possibly a relative.
Rider + Gypsy Woman	Determined, independent woman in control of her life.
Gypsy Woman + Clover	A woman who brings trouble.
Clover + Gypsy Woman	Difficulties with a woman.
Gypsy Woman + Ship	A distant woman coming slowly.
Ship + Gypsy Woman	Displacement for or with a woman.
Gypsy Woman + House	Mother, grandmother, aunt, mistress of the house.
House + Gypsy Woman	Balanced, structured woman.
Gypsy Woman + Tree	Woman who heals, doctor, connected to medical area.
Tree + Gypsy Woman	Sick woman. Physical, emotional and spiritual diseases.
Gypsy Woman + Cloud	Unstable woman, confused, indecisive.
Cloud + Gypsy Woman	Woman who hides her true self, fake.
Gypsy + Snake	Seductive, sensual and sexual woman
Snake + Gypsy Woman	Betrayal by a woman.
Gypsy Woman + Coffin	Sick woman, depressed, unsatisfied, cheater.
Coffin + Gypsy Woman	Changes and transformations for or in a woman.
Gypsy Woman + Bouquet	Beautiful, happy and attractive woman.
Bouquet + Gypsy Woman	Happiness, success, balance from a woman.
Gypsy Woman + Sickle	Decisive woman, confident and taking the lead.
Sickle + Gypsy Woman	**Woman leaving your life, separation.**
Gypsy Woman + Whip	Woman bound to spirituality. Witch, magician.
Whip + Gypsy Woman	Persistent, active, agile, sexual woman.
Gypsy Woman + Birds	Communicative woman, happy, agitated.
Birds + Gypsy Woman	Gossip from or about a woman.
Gypsy Woman + Child	Immature, young, inconsequential woman.
Child + Gypsy Woman	Beginning of a new life with a woman.
Gypsy Woman + Fox	Crafty, intelligent, manipulative woman.
Fox + Gypsy Woman	Alert for or about a woman.
Gypsy Woman + Bear	Protective, domineering, jealous, possessive woman.
Bear + Gypsy Woman	Success for a woman or coming from a woman.
Gypsy Woman + Star	Spiritualized woman, medium. Blood gypsy.
Star + Gypsy Woman	Spiritual mentor or spiritual gypsy.
Gypsy Woman + Stork	Flexible, open-minded woman.
Stork + Gypsy Woman	Changes and news for or about a woman. Pregnancy.
Gypsy Woman + Dog	Faithful woman, friend, companion, trustworthy, cordial.

Dog + Gypsy Woman	Friends acting on behalf of a woman. Female friendship.
Gypsy Woman + Tower	Lonely woman, arrogant, spiritual.
Tower + Gypsy Woman	Woman from the past.
Gypsy Woman + Garden	Public, sociable, popular woman.
Garden + Gypsy Woman	Plans made with a woman.
Gypsy Woman + Mountain	Difficult woman, cold, indifferent.
Mountain + Gypsy Woman	Problems and difficulties with a woman.
Gypsy Woman + Path	Indecisive woman, unsteady, hesitant.
Path + Gypsy Woman	Options for or with a woman.
Gypsy Woman + Rat	Exhausted woman, tired, depressed. Thief.
Rat + Gypsy Woman	Weariness or theft from or provoked by a woman.
Gypsy Woman + Heart	Woman in love, emotional, sentimental.
Heart + Gypsy Woman	Feelings by or from a woman.
Gypsy Woman + Ring	Married, committed woman.
Ring + Gypsy Woman	Union, relationship, partnership with a woman.
Gypsy Woman + Book	Studious woman, intelligent, dedicated, revealing.
Book + Gypsy Woman	Secrets about or coming from a woman.
Gypsy Woman + Letter	Communicative woman.
Letter + Gypsy Woman	Warnings or messages coming through or from a woman.
Gypsy Woman + Man	Woman with masculine personality.
Gypsy Man + Woman	**Relationship, engagement, a proposal on the way.**
Gypsy Woman + Lily	Mature, elderly, quiet, patient woman.
Lily + Gypsy Woman	Peace, tranquillity, retirement coming to a woman.
Gypsy Woman + Sun	Successful, progressive and healthy woman.
Sun + Gypsy Woman	Success in all areas for a woman.
Gypsy Woman + Moon	Creative woman, intuitive, mysterious, spiritual.
Moon + Gypsy Woman	Achievements for, with a woman.
Gypsy Woman + Key	Reliable woman who finds solutions.
Key + Gypsy Woman	Solutions coming to or from a woman.
Gypsy Woman + Fish	Financially successful, prosperous, materialistic woman.
Fish + Gypsy Woman	Financial prosperity for a woman.
Gypsy Woman + Anchor	Confident, stable woman, who takes time to act.
Anchor + Gypsy Woman	Security with or for a woman.
Gypsy Woman + Cross	Religious woman, overwhelmed or one who is suffering.
Cross + Gypsy Woman	Delayed completion for a woman.

Card 30 - The Lily

Lily + Rider	Use wisdom and cool to deal with the upcoming phase.
Rider + Lily	A period of peace, tranquillity and growth in the emotional area.
Lily + Clover	Emotional coldness bringing trouble.
Clover + Lily	Problems in having peace and happiness.
Lily + Ship	Change of place causing coldness in the situation.
Ship + Lily	Long-distance travel.
Lily + House	Find more wisdom in family relationships.
House + Lily	Old house/property. Property of family heirloom.
Lily + Tree	Wisdom and a certain coldness bringing growth.
Tree + Lily	Sexual health, sexual disease.
Lily + Cloud	Lack of wisdom in a situation.
Cloud + Lily	Unrest, loss of peace.
Lily + Snake	Intense sexual relationship.
Snake + Lily	Sexual desire, sexual attraction.
Lily + Coffin	Tranquillity bringing a great turnaround.
Coffin + Lily	Loss of tranquillity. Rupture, separation.
Lily + Bouquet	Expanded happiness.
Bouquet + Lily	Harmony and contentment. Peace.
Lily + Sickle	Maturity that brings positive results.
Sickle + Lily	Separation or unrest.
Lily + Whip	Peace and tranquillity at risk.
Whip + Lily	Physical tiredness. Middle age.
Lily + Birds	Peace from the wisdom of life. Union of peace.
Birds + Lily	Long discussions. Mature discussions bringing results.
Lily + Child	Premature, rushed marriage.
Child + Lily	Peaceful, calm child, who brings peace.
Lily + Fox	Use strategy and maturity in negotiations.
Fox + Lily	Personality well defined, well resolved.
Lily + Bear	Peace and lasting happiness.
Bear + Lily	Prosperity acquired during life.
Lily + Star	Something that keeps fame under control, is not dazzled.
Star + Lily	Success that comes from the past.
Lily + Stork	Coldness causing changes.
Stork + Lily	Sentient, balanced news.

Lily + Dog	Coldness in a friendship.
Dog + Lily	Wise friend, important, from long ago.
Lily + Tower	Spiritual wisdom.
Tower + Lily	Inner peace, peace with yourself.
Lily + Garden	Coldness and social distancing.
Garden + Lily	Safe, reliable, mature plans.
Lily + Mountain	**Isolation to find wisdom and justice.**
Mountain + Lily	Lack of wisdom, of sexual life, of peace.
Lily + Path	Stay cool to decide. Use wisdom to decide.
Path + Lily	Paths of peace, tranquillity and maturity.
Lily + Rat	Problems in or of old age.
Rat + Lily	End of an unofficial relationship.
Lily + Heart	Emotional maturity.
Heart + Lily	Cold and calculating feelings.
Lily + Ring	Coldness in marriage, partnership, relationship.
Ring + Lily	Serious, mature relationship.
Lily + Book	Expert in your professional field.
Book + Lily	Ancient secrets.
Lily + Letter	Use wisdom with documents, warnings, messages.
Letter + Lily	Old documents or old news.
Lily + Gypsy Man	Peace, tranquillity, retirement coming to a man.
Gypsy Man + Lily	Mature, elderly, quiet, patient man.
Lily + Gypsy Woman	Peace, tranquillity, retirement coming to a woman.
Gypsy Woman + Lily	Mature, elderly, quiet, patient woman.
Lily + Sun	Peace that brings progress and growth.
Sun + Lily	Late success.
Lily + Moon	Personal growth, self-development. Maturity.
Moon + Lily	Emotional security. Romance with an older person.
Lily + Key	Certainty in the solutions found.
Key + Lily	Mature solution that brings peace and tranquillity.
Lily + Fish	Financial tranquillity. Stability.
Fish + Lily	Honest business and money.
Lily + Anchor	Wisdom, tranquillity and long-term peace.
Anchor + Lily	Stagnation. It takes time to evolve.
Lily + Cross	Unfulfilling sex, without pleasure.
Cross + Lily	Lack of peace and tranquillity.

Card 31 - The Sun

Sun + Rider	Do not run away from reality, do not hide.
Rider + Sun	A new phase of realizations, projects fulfilled, dreams realized.
Sun + Clover	Clear solution to resolve difficulties.
Clover + Sun	Problems that cannot be hidden.
Sun + Ship	New horizons, success.
Ship + Sun	Travel overseas.
Sun + House	Clarity in the family relationship.
House + Sun	Family in the phase of happiness.
Sun + Tree	Physical, emotional and spiritual healing.
Tree + Sun	Situation of strength and happiness.
Sun + Cloud	Accept what cannot be changed.
Cloud + Sun	Lack of clarity, thoughts and vision.
Sun + Snake	Face a difficult situation.
Snake + Sun	Agility bringing success. Situation resolution.
Sun + Coffin	Total renovation.
Coffin + Sun	Loss of energy, discouragement.
Sun + Bouquet	Perfection.
Bouquet + Sun	Celebration of great success.
Sun + Sickle	Quick success without much stability.
Sickle + Sun	End of success.
Sun + Whip	Pleasure in sex.
Whip + Sun	Competition for power.
Sun + Birds	Stability of emotions and feelings.
Birds + Sun	Definitive resolution coming from conversations.
Sun + Child	Promising start. Future vision.
Child + Sun	Desired and scheduled pregnancy. Restless child.
Sun + Fox	Misleading, false success.
Fox + Sun	Pay attention to things that are obvious. Open your eyes.
Sun + Bear	Great prosperity, success, social elevation.
Bear + Sun	Clear, visible evil.
Sun + Star	Gypsy spirituality. Success and prestige.
Star + Sun	Gypsy spirituality. Dreams come true, fame, good luck.
Sun + Stork	Positivity favouring transformations. Energy on the rise.
Stork + Sun	Pregnancy.

Sun + Dog	Great friendship, great loyalty.
Dog + Sun	True friendship. Reciprocal friendship.
Sun + Tower	Ancient spirituality, of other lives, of birth.
Tower + Sun	Solitude that brings personal evolution.
Sun + Garden	Public success. Social highlight.
Garden + Sun	Great success, magnification of positivity.
Sun + Mountain	Face your problems.
Mountain + Sun	Success happens, despite problems.
Sun + Path	Great event.
Path + Sun	Correct, successful choices.
Sun + Rat	Great annoyance.
Rat + Sun	Loss of energy, anaemia, weakness, illness.
Sun + Heart	Sexual romance, new love, passion.
Heart + Sun	**Feelings that cannot be avoided, true love.**
Sun + Ring	Making the relationship official.
Ring + Sun	Partnership, relationship, successful union.
Sun + Book	Secrets coming to the surface, being discovered.
Book + Sun	Successful professional. Important studies.
Sun + Letter	Great news.
Letter + Sun	Documents that solve issues, bring success.
Sun + Gypsy Man	Successful man in all aspects.
Gypsy Man + Sun	Successful, progressive, healthy man.
Sun + Gypsy Woman	Success in all areas for a woman.
Gypsy Woman + Sun	Successful, progressive, healthy woman.
Sun + Lily	Late success.
Lily + Sun	Peace that brings progress and growth.
Sun + Moon	Success with creativity.
Moon + Sun	Spiritual achievements. Gypsy spirits.
Sun + Key	Success opening more growth options.
Key + Sun	Openings for progress and success.
Sun + Fish	Large amount of money arriving. Thriving financially.
Fish + Sun	Materiality acting on success.
Sun + Anchor	Objectives achieved permanently.
Anchor + Sun	Safe success.
Sun + Cross	Energy to finalize the question.
Cross + Sun	Karmic success.

Card 32 - The Moon

Moon + Rider	Intuition quickly bringing new directions into a situation.
Rider + Moon	Look within yourself for answers and intuitive paths.
Moon + Clover	Intuition showing the problems.
Clover + Moon	Difficulty in connecting to the spiritual.
Moon + Ship	Travel by own merit.
Ship + Moon	Romantic Journey.
Moon + House	Deserved property.
House + Moon	Property or house of dreams.
Moon + Tree	Secret meeting, hidden.
Tree + Moon	Spiritual security.
Moon + Cloud	Achievements without merit.
Cloud + Moon	Uncertainty of thoughts.
Moon + Snake	**Results achieved through betrayal.**
Snake + Moon	Disappointments, loss of what was guaranteed.
Moon + Coffin	Dreams and plans made.
Coffin + Moon	Loss of creativity, mental illness.
Moon + Bouquet	Deserved satisfaction and success.
Bouquet + Moon	Keep feelings more guarded, hidden.
Moon + Sickle	Positive cuts made by desire itself.
Sickle + Moon	Loss of intuition.
Moon + Whip	Great magic, magic that brings results.
Whip + Moon	May indicate magic, work done, conflict.
Moon + Birds	Conquering through partnership and communication.
Birds + Moon	Creative, intuitive conversations.
Moon + Child	Pregnancy and birth after many attempts.
Child + Moon	Spiritual child.
Moon + Fox	Degrading situation.
Fox + Moon	Wrong handling of spiritual things.
Moon + Bear	Individual progress, loneliness.
Bear + Moon	Self-protection, someone who protects, something guaranteed
Moon + Star	Gypsy spirits. Hide success.
Star + Moon	Gypsy spirituality. Very well-deserved success.
Moon + Stork	Personal success sought.
Stork + Moon	News sought, deserved.

Moon + Dog	Achievements with loyal friends.
Dog + Moon	Guides, teachers, spiritual friends.
Moon + Tower	Lonely achievements, only yours.
Tower + Moon	Emotional internalization to find ways to achieve things.
Moon + Garden	Social recognition.
Garden + Moon	Mystic event.
Moon + Mountain	Hidden enemy. Confusion and fears.
Mountain + Moon	Problems to get what you deserve.
Moon + Path	**Deserved and relaxed path.**
Path + Moon	Decisions based on the emotional.
Moon + Rat	Fraudulent achievements.
Rat + Moon	Depression, insecurity, insomnia.
Moon + Heart	Feelings hidden, guarded.
Heart + Moon	Romance that can turn into something lasting.
Moon + Ring	Emotional, spiritual, strong connection.
Ring + Moon	Union, agreement, successful social circle.
Moon + Book	Professional promotion. Growth coming from studies.
Book + Moon	Secret, hidden.
Moon + Letter	Official success, disclosed.
Letter + Moon	Message, communication, warning, anonymous news.
Moon + Gypsy Man	Achievements for, with or of a man.
Gypsy Man + Moon	Creative man, intuitive, mysterious, spiritual.
Moon + Gypsy Woman	Success in all areas for a woman.
Gypsy Woman + Moon	Successful, progressive, healthy woman.
Moon + Lily	Emotional security. Romance with an older person.
Lily + Moon	Personal growth, self-development. Maturity.
Moon + Sun	Spiritual achievements. Gypsy spirits.
Sun + Moon	Success with creativity.
Moon + Key	Deserved solution, of its own merit. Look for the solutions inside.
Key + Moon	You cannot see the options and solutions. Hidden or creative solutions.
Moon + Fish	Merits or success in business. Financial recognition.
Fish + Moon	Financial gains that come from creativity.
Moon + Anchor	Long-term merit.
Anchor + Moon	Stuck and hidden.
Moon + Cross	Triumph, conquest via self-struggle.

Cross + Moon   Faith for matters that flee from normality.

Card 33 - The Key

Key + Rider	Whatever was hidden is now discovered, new beginnings.
Rider + Key	Seek new solutions to life.
Key + Clover	Solving problems.
Clover + Key	Problems in the solutions of a situation.
Key + Ship	Solving problems to move around.
Ship + Key	Solutions change.
Key + House	New house.
Home + Key	Family help with solutions.
Key + Tree	Seek new ways of growth.
Tree + Key	Growth by expanding solutions.
Key + Cloud	Solutions to clear ideas. Therapy.
Cloud + Key	Confused thoughts do not allow finding solutions.
Key + Snake	**Discovery of betrayal.**
Snake + Key	Acting fast to get the solutions.
Key + Coffin	Seek solutions, act to change.
Coffin + Key	Positive changes, solutions.
Key + Bouquet	Perfect solution, indisputable.
Bouquet + Key	Discovering the path of happiness.
Key + Sickle	Important, definitive decision.
Sickle + Key	**Erase the need to find solutions.**
Key + Whip	Necessary decision making.
Whip + Key	Discussion in search of a solution.
Key + Birds	The solution lies in communication.
Birds + Key	Socialize to find options.
Key + Child	Immature and childish solutions.
Child + Key	Phase of search for solutions.
Key + Fox	Undo traps, manipulations.
Fox + Key	Plan to find solutions.
Key + Bear	Solving problems in a selfish way.
Bear + Key	Finding solutions, mastering options.
Key + Star	Open your own spirituality.
Star + Key	Prize, to win things.
Key + Stork	Discovering a surprise.
Stork + Key	News that show solutions.

Key + Dog	Creating new friends, expanding the social circle.
Dog + Key	Loyalty that makes decisions, opens options.
Key + Tower	Changing the solitary phase, opening options to relate.
Tower + Key	Looking for solutions in the past.
Key + Garden	Discoveries with solutions.
Garden + Key	Heal through alternative medicine.
Key + Mountain	Overcoming and solving difficulties.
Mountain + Key	Problems in the solutions found.
Key + Path	Solution or path opening. Open to the public.
Path + Key	Various means of solving, various solutions.
Key + Rat	Search useless, negative.
Rat + Key	Struggling to find solutions.
Key + Heart	Emotional solutions.
Heart + Key	Someone will open their heart, feelings will be revealed.
Key + Ring	Solve the union, the relationship, the society.
Ring + Key	Agreement made, relationship becoming official.
Key + Book	Professional solutions.
Book + Key	Secret revealed.
Key + Letter	Solutions are in communications, warnings and documents.
Letter + Key	Notice of something being solved.
Key + Gypsy Man	Solutions coming from a man.
Gypsy Man + Key	Trusted man, who solves.
Key + Gypsy Woman	Solutions coming to or from a woman.
Gypsy Woman + Key	Reliable woman who finds solutions.
Key + Lily	Mature solution that brings peace and tranquillity.
Lily + Key	Certainty in the solutions found.
Key + Sun	Openings for progress and success.
Sun + Key	Success opening more growth options.
Key + Moon	You cannot see the options and solutions. Hidden or creative solutions.
Moon + Key	Deserved solution, of its own merit. Look for the solutions inside.
Key + Fish	Solutions bringing wealth and financial prosperity.
Fish + Key	Diversified financial investments.
Key + Anchor	Secure solutions.
Anchor + Key	Locked in options.
Key + Cross	Varied options of victory and finalization.

Cross + Key   Spiritual solutions, coming from spirituality.

Card 34 - The Fish

Fish + Rider	Money arriving. Prosperity coming quickly.
Rider + Fish	Seek material progress, go after financial goals.
Fish + Clover	The material world bringing problems.
Clover + Fish	Financial problems.
Fish + Ship	Expensive trip.
Ship + Fish	Travel or displacement bringing prosperity.
Fish + House	Family financial growth coming up.
House + Fish	Prosperous family, large family.
Fish + Tree	Cash input bringing growth.
Tree + Fish	Seek stability to have prosperity.
Fish + Cloud	Financial uncertainties, unfavourable financial matters.
Cloud + Fish	Materialistic thinking. Hidden money.
Fish + Snake	Material and financial problems.
Snake + Fish	**Betrayal with money.**
Fish + Coffin	Financial loss, change of status.
Coffin + Fish	Could be a funeral, change of life.
Fish + Bouquet	Financial situation bringing balance and success.
Bouquet + Fish	Gift of value, expensive.
Fish + Sickle	Money that yields, investment.
Sickle + Fish	Loss of money, status, social position.
Fish + Whip	Greed. Diversify investments.
Whip + Fish	Contrary to money.
Fish + Birds	Momentary, fleeting prosperity.
Birds + Fish	Financial speculation, illicit money.
Fish + Child	Materiality, booming prosperity.
Child + Fish	Small amount of money coming.
Fish + Fox	Corruption, misuse of money.
Fox + Fish	Financial trap.
Fish + Bear	Trapped by the domination of another person.
Bear + Fish	Take a breath to be able to thrive financially.
Fish + Star	Prosperity, fame, success, brilliance itself.
Star + Fish	Financial success.
Fish + Stork	Fast arrival of news.
Stork + Fish	Changing in the financial situation.
Fish + Dog	Friendship for financial interest.

Dog + Fish	Financial partner, business partner.
Fish + Tower	Great solitude and detachment.
Tower + Fish	Spirituality is being used for financial purposes.
Fish + Garden	Growth, enlargement, great prosperity.
Garden + Fish	Magnification of materiality. Increase of customers.
Fish + Mountain	Prosperity that takes time to happen.
Mountain + Fish	Financial and material problems.
Fish + Path	Money entering through more than one source.
Path + Fish	Paths of prosperity.
Fish + Rat	Illicit money, conquered in the wrong way.
Rat + Fish	Theft of money, goods.
Fish + Heart	Person or materialistic situation, attached to money.
Heart + Fish	Material and financial satisfaction.
Fish + Ring	Prosperity bringing unity.
Ring + Fish	Financial, material relationship.
Fish + Book	Investment in the professional life or studies.
Book + Fish	Well paid job.
Fish + Letter	Prosperity where documents are involved, inheritance or settlement.
Letter + Fish	Financial documents. Bank account.
Fish + Gypsy Man	Financial prosperity for a man.
Gypsy Man + Fish	Financially successful, prosperous, materialistic man.
Fish + Gypsy Woman	Financial prosperity for a woman.
Gypsy Woman + Fish	Financially successful, prosperous, materialistic woman.
Fish + Lily	Honest business and money.
Lily + Fish	Financial tranquillity. Stability.
Fish + Sun	Materiality acting on success.
Sun + Fish	Large amount of money arriving. Thriving financially.
Fish + Moon	Financial gains that come from creativity.
Moon + Fish	Merits or success in business. Financial recognition.
Fish + Key	Diversified financial investments.
Key + Fish	Solutions bringing wealth and financial prosperity.
Fish + Anchor	Long-term financial application. Safe money.
Anchor + Fish	Stuck finding a solution to a financial question.
Fish + Cross	Investments ending a difficult issue that was causing suffering.
Cross + Fish	End of materiality, of prosperity, of money.

Card 35 - The Anchor

Anchor + Rider	The security you are looking for will arrive quickly.
Rider + Anchor	New things will not come if there is no movement.
Anchor + Clover	Attachment to problems.
Clover + Anchor	Security issues.
Anchor + Ship	Security providing travel.
Ship + Anchor	Travel stopped, boring.
Anchor + House	Stable family.
House + Anchor	Trapped in a family situation.
Anchor + Tree	Safety that brings growth.
Tree + Anchor	Safe growth. Stable health.
Anchor + Cloud	Great mental instability.
Cloud + Anchor	Thoughts affecting safety.
Anchor + Snake	Stable relationship with a lover.
Snake + Anchor	**Betrayal and insecurity.**
Anchor + Coffin	Transformations are stuck and do not happen.
Coffin + Anchor	Loss of stability.
Anchor + Bouquet	Goals achieved.
Bouquet + Anchor	Enduring happiness that does not end.
Anchor + Sickle	Security brought by planning.
Sickle + Anchor	Definitive end.
Anchor + Whip	Stuck in the painful situation. No change in suffering.
Whip + Anchor	Difficulties in stability.
Anchor + Birds	A confused conversation that does not evolve or result in a solution.
Birds + Anchor	Stable relationship. Feelings of permanent happiness.
Anchor + Child	Restrain children, grandchildren, nephews, nieces more.
Child + Anchor	New phase of security and stability.
Anchor + Fox	Trapped.
Fox + Anchor	Ancient dishonesty which persists, rooted.
Anchor + Bear	**Feeling of domination from another person.**
Bear + Anchor	Grumpy person, stuck in his/her own ideas.
Anchor + Star	Stuck in self.
Star + Anchor	Long-term fame.
Anchor + Stork	Stagnation, nothing new.
Stork + Anchor	Improved safety.

Anchor + Dog	Feeling trapped by friendships. Stopped, not evolving.
Dog + Anchor	Stable, lasting friendship.
Anchor + Tower	Spiritual security.
Tower + Anchor	Stuck in a self-imposed solitude.
Anchor + Garden	Stability and social tranquillity.
Garden + Anchor	Extending security.
Anchor + Mountain	Security will help overcome difficulties.
Mountain + Anchor	Obstacles that linger.
Anchor + Path	Locked in options, choices.
Path + Anchor	Decisions taken safely.
Anchor + Rat	Stress is settling.
Rat + Anchor	Lack of balance and safety.
Anchor + Heart	Emotional prison.
Heart + Anchor	Deep and secure feelings.
Anchor + Ring	Feeling pressured in an engagement.
Ring + Anchor	Stable, secure, old relationship.
Anchor + Book	Professional security.
Book + Anchor	Well guarded secret, difficult to discover.
Anchor + Letter	Stagnation waiting for documents.
Letter + Anchor	Safe and reliable notices.
Anchor + Gypsy Man	Security with a man.
Gypsy Man + Anchor	A reliable, stable man who takes time to act.
Anchor + Gypsy Woman	Security with a woman.
Gypsy Woman + Anchor	Confident, stable woman, who takes time to act.
Anchor + Lily	Stagnation. It takes time to evolve.
Lily + Anchor	Wisdom, tranquillity and long-term peace.
Anchor + Sun	Safe success.
Sun + Anchor	Objectives achieved permanently.
Anchor + Moon	Stuck and hidden.
Moon + Anchor	Long-term merit.
Anchor + Key	Locked in options.
Key + Anchor	Secure solutions.
Anchor + Fish	Stuck finding a solution to a financial question.
Fish + Anchor	Long-term financial application. Safe money.
Anchor + Cross	Stuck in a situation. Regrets.
Cross + Anchor	Safe, intended finish.

Card 36 - The Cross

Cross + Rider	All that had to be surpassed has been. Now the happy ending arrives.
Rider + Cross	Seek to overcome difficulties and pains.
Cross + Clover	End of problems.
Clover + Cross	Proof of faith.
Cross + Ship	End of situation bringing slow changes.
Ship + Cross	Journey of faith, in search of faith.
Cross + House	Family victory.
House + Cross	Church, religious space.
Cross + Tree	**Endings that bring security.**
Tree + Cross	Person, situation of great faith. Frequent physical pain.
Cross + Cloud	Uncertain victory.
Cloud + Cross	Lack of faith, spiritual doubts.
Cross + Snake	Faith being put to the test.
Snake + Cross	Difficult and dangerous journey.
Cross + Coffin	Aggravation of disease, worsening of health.
Coffin + Cross	Changes with victories.
Cross + Bouquet	Happy destiny.
Bouquet + Cross	To give, to do something for someone else, charity.
Cross + Sickle	Volunteer work.
Sickle + Cross	**Get rid of predicable ideas.**
Cross + Whip	Path with more difficulty, challenge, difficult lesson.
Whip + Cross	End of suffering, abuse and/or physical aggression.
Cross + Birds	End, disruption of negotiations. Breakdown of communication.
Birds + Cross	Difficult communication but ending a situation.
Cross + Child	Completion of a phase to start a new one.
Child + Cross	Difficult childhood. Child going through depression.
Cross + Fox	End of a dangerous and manipulative situation.
Fox + Cross	Stuck in lies and deceit.
Cross + Bear	Completion of something that took a long time, no return.
Bear + Cross	Still fighting for the happy ending.
Cross + Star	**Destiny karma, soulmates.**
Star + Cross	Spiritual thoughts, of faith, of God.

Cross + Stork	Plans changed, unwanted change.
Stork + Cross	Difficult changes.
Cross + Dog	Overcoming and finishing something with the help of friends.
Dog + Cross	Difficult friendship that makes you suffer, hurt.
Cross + Tower	Decision, choice, struggle for isolation, for solitude.
Tower + Cross	Religious site, temple, church, centre.
Cross + Garden	Completion of projects and plans.
Garden + Cross	Group based on faith, spiritual, social aid.
Cross + Mountain	More problems after resolving the current situation.
Mountain + Cross	Deep depression.
Cross + Path	Difficulty to choose, to walk, to act.
Path + Cross	Destiny.
Cross + Rat	Great loss.
Rat + Cross	Deep weariness in faith.
Cross + Heart	End of a feeling, of an emotion.
Heart + Cross	Faith in every way.
Cross + Ring	End of a relationship after much suffering.
Ring + Cross	Difficult relationship.
Cross + Book	Difficulty to keep a secret, a burden that hurts.
Book + Cross	Studies or religious work.
Cross + Letter	Finalization of documentation that took a long time.
Letter + Cross	Spiritual notice.
Cross + Gypsy Man	Delayed completion for a man.
Gypsy Man + Cross	Religious man, overwhelmed or one who is suffering.
Cross + Gypsy Woman	Delayed completion for a woman.
Gypsy Woman + Cross	Religious woman, overwhelmed or one who is suffering.
Cross + Lily	Lack of peace and tranquillity.
Lily + Cross	Unfulfilling sex, without pleasure.
Cross + Sun	Karmic success.
Sun + Cross	Energy to finalize the question.
Cross + Moon	Faith for matters that escape normality.
Moon + Cross	Triumph, conquest via self-struggle.
Cross + Key	Spiritual solutions, coming from spirituality.
Key + Cross	Varied options of victory and finalization.
Cross + Fish	End of materiality, of prosperity, of money.

Fish + Cross	Investments ending a difficult issue that was causing suffering.
Cross + Anchor	Safe, intended end.
Anchor + Cross	Stuck in a situation. Regrets.

About the author

Rodrigo Petrosky is a qualified counsellor, coach, inspirational speaker, author, psychotherapist specializing in relationships, breakup recovery, post abortion syndrome, eating disorders and men's mental health.

Rodrigo holds Masters Degree in Counselling, Post Graduate Diploma in Education, Post Graduate Diploma in Human Resources, Bachelor in Business and Bachelor in Psychology.

Rodrigo is proficient in several modalities and has experience in private practice, army counselling, corrections, disability, mental health, immigration and education. Rodrigo has hosted a number of events, spoke at conferences and festivals. He is the founder of Impact Balance and Wellbeing counselling service and has introduced an innovative therapeutic cooking group. Rodrigo has also been involved in a number of charity and nonprofit ventures.

Rodrigo is originally from Brazil from a mix of Russian, Iberian and Romani background. He lived in 7 different countries and speaks several languages. From early age Rodrigo was exposed to Gypsy healing, clairvoyance and shamanic medicine. Rodrigo has practiced martial arts for 10 years. In his work Rodrigo combines spirituality with evidence-based approaches.

Life challenges have taken Rodrigo on a full journey of recovery and resilience. After a near death experience he has gone through a full spiritual awakening and has helped thousands of people.

About the illustrator

Dr. Anastasia Globa is a researcher, academic and designer working in the fields of architecture and art, with strong research interests in algorithmic design, immersive environments and advanced manufacturing.

Anastasia was born in Russia, where she has completed her initial studies in classical arts (drawing, painting, sculpting and digital design) and architecture. She then moved to Germany (Dessau, Bauhaus) where she continued her studies in architecture and design at Master level. The doctoral research work (New Zealand, 2015) and most of teaching, done in the span of 10 years in New Zealand, Russia and Australia focused on the use computation, algorithmic form-making and digital fabrication. Throughout the years Anastasia continued her creative work, being engaged in various exhibitions, life drawing sessions, design competitions, public events and projects, keeping her painting and sketching as an enjoyable but mostly non-profit hobby.

During the three years of her post-doc-research fellowship (2015-2018) Anastasia has further extended her skillset and developed a large number of projects using interactive Virtual (VR) and Augmented (AR) environments. VR and AR was applied in projects involving design exploration, data visualization and pre-occupancy simulation. She worked as a key member of the Interdisciplinary Design Laboratory at Deakin University and she has vast experience with the development and testing of digital and physical prototypes, interdisciplinary design and industry collaborations.

The Gypsy Cards project was something 'out-of-pattern' activity that utilized her design and drawing skills (both hand-drawn and digital) and required abundance of creativity. It was an amazing experience that involved rigorous research, trial-and-error and massive amount of time and effort but was also highly rewarding and satisfactory.

Bibliography

Azevdo, Aluizio (2015). Anais do IV Colóquio Semiótica das Mídias. vol. 4, n° 1. Japaratinga, AL: UFAL, 2015
Jurua, Padrinho (2015). Oraculos Utilizados pelo Povo Cigano. Alfabeto. Sao Paulo - Brasil.
Mathews, Caitlin (1952). The Complete Lenormand Oracle handbook. - Reading the Language and Symbols of the Cards. Destiny Books. Rochester. USA
McKee, Ramona (2013). Madame Lenormand and Her Cards (The Bit of Study Series)
Sayer, Mandy (2017). Australian Gypsies – Their Secret History. Griffin Press. Sydney
Tchileva, Druzhemira (2004-11-16). Emerging Romani Voices from Latin America European Roma Rights Centre.
Teorema, Angus (1997) Portugal (In Portuguese)
Touchkoff, Svetlana (1991). Russian Gypsy Fortune Telling Cards. Harper Collins. New York.
Ramanoush, Nicolas (2015). Os Segredos dos Oraculos Ciganos. (In Portuguese). Embaixada Cigana no Brasil. Sao Paulo - Brasil.
Superinteressante Magazine (2016) A Saga dos Ciganos - Luciano Marsiglia (In Portuguese). Brazil.

Order your Gypsy Card deck at whitelightshop.com.

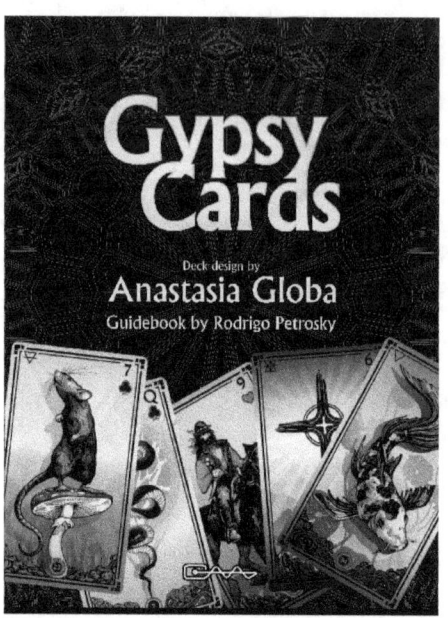

www.ingramcontent.com/pod-product-compliance
Lightning Source LLC
Chambersburg PA
CBHW071905290426
44110CB00013B/1284